ms should be returned on or befor
own below. Items not already requ
rrowers may be renewed in person,
lephone. To renew, please quote the number on the
rcode label. To renew on line a PIN is required.
is can be requested at your local library.
new online @ **www.dublincitypubliclibraries.ie**
les charged for overdue items will include postage
curred in recovery. Damage to or loss of items will be
arged to the borrower.

Leabharlanna Poiblí Chathair Bhaile Átha Cliath
Dublin City Public Libraries

Dublin City
Baile Átha Cliath

Brainse Rátheanaigh
Raheny Branch
Tel: 8315521

Date Due	Date Due	Date Due
2 0 NOV 2018		

THE
LITTLE
BOOK
OF
MERRION
AND
BOOTERSTOWN

HUGH ORAM

The
History
Press
Ireland

First published 2018

The History Press Ireland
50 City Quay
Dublin 2
Ireland
www.thehistorypress.ie

British Library Cataloguing in Publication Data.
A catalogue record for this book is available from the British Library.

ISBN 978 0 7509 8766 0

Typesetting and origination by The History Press
Printed and bound by TJ International Ltd

CONTENTS

ACKNOWLEDGEMENTS

First of all, I'd especially like to thank my dear wife Bernadette for all the help, encouragement and support she's given over the past forty years while I've been writing books. I'd also like to thank good friends who've also given me lots of support in my literary endeavours, particularly Thelma Byrne, Dublin; Aisling Curley, Dublin; Miriam Doyle, Co. Dublin; Maria Gillen, Athlone; and Mary J. Murphy, Caherlistrane, Co. Galway.

Thanks to Catherine KilBride, who lives in Merrion, for all her help with historical material on the district; Charles Lysaght, another Merrion resident, for his insights on Merrion; Caroline Mullan of the archives department of Blackrock College; Monica Lynott of St Andrew's College, Booterstown, and Susan Roundtree, a specialist on Irish brickwork. As always, the Pembroke Library in Anglesea Road, Dublin 4, the Gilbert Library in Pearse Street, Dublin 2, the Dún Laoghaire-Rathdown County Council library service and the National Library of Ireland have been useful sources of information.

I would also like to thank the following for their assistance: Noelle Dowling, diocesan archivist, Archdiocese of Dublin; Ailbhe De Groot of Sweet, Booterstown Avenue; Dave Downes, Dublin Book Browsers, Stillorgan; Joe O'Rorke, owner, and Lar Flynn of the Old Punch Bowl, Booterstown; Firthjof Berndsen, German Embassy, Booterstown; Brown's newsagents, Merrion Road, Merrion; Gleeson's pub, Booterstown Avenue; Paola Macari, Petit, Merrion Road, Merrion; Jim and John McCabe of McCabe's wines and restaurant, Foxrock; Mick McCabe, An Post museum and archive section; Brian O'Brien, Books on the Green, Sandymount; and Peter Pearson, Co. Wexford.

I'm also indebted to the technical contributions of Dean Lochner of the Bondi Group in Ballsbridge, Dublin, and to the work of artist Nick Fegan in creating the line drawings for the book.

INTRODUCTION

Merrion and Booterstown are two of the most select districts in south Co. Dublin, two suburbs that have long been residential districts but which in recent decades have seen much development.

Both lie on the Merrion Road, which continues as the Rock Road through Williamstown to Blackrock; this is now one of the main traffic arteries of south Co. Dublin, with considerable volumes of traffic at morning and evening rush hours. Running close to the sea is the main railway line from Dublin to Wexford and Rosslare, which is also much used by DART services travelling as far as Greystones, Co. Wicklow.

Merrion traces its history back to the foundation of Merrion Castle in the early fourteenth century and gets its name from an Irish word for seashore, while Booterstown is also traced back to the fourteenth century, when it was called Ballybothyr, because it was on the road to Dunleary. Later, it became known as Butterstown.

In the nineteenth century, two establishments were founded that have since had a profound impact on the people they serve. First was the setting up of St Mary's on the Merrion Road to provide a home for blind people as well as schooling for younger blind pupils. That opened in 1868, followed the year after by St John's Anglican retirement home, which in its earlier days provided shelter for retired maids and other servants. At the time of writing (2018) St John's is undergoing a tremendous expansion of its facilities.

St Vincent's University Hospital has been functioning at Merrion since 1970, when the hospital moved from its original site at St Stephen's Green in the city centre. In recent years, the new St Vincent's Private Hospital has also been making its own contribution to increased medical facilities in the area.

In terms of residential development, Merrion has been somewhat limited; although the area between the Merrion Road and the Strand Road, facing the sea, has long been a residential area, with the addition in more recent decades of the Merrion Village apartments just off the Merrion Road. Many houses, often dating back to the nineteenth century, line the Merrion Road as it passes through Merrion. The vast new housing and office developments at Elm Park have added a new dimension to the district, although many local people are critical of their sheer scale.

It's a sign of how recently Merrion has been in the ascendant that the huge Catholic church on the Merrion Road, Our Lady Queen of Peace, was only consecrated in 1953, replacing an earlier, temporary building fashioned from timber, known as the Tin Church because it had a tin roof. The vast car park beside the church was in the news for a different reason: A new road was proposed, linking Strand Road with Merrion Road, in order to bypass the congestion at the Merrion Gates, with underpasses for pedestrians and cyclists. The proposal generated such enormous controversy that its construction has since been shelved indefinitely.

In terms of retail, the biggest impact in the district has come from the Merrion Shopping Centre, now just over thirty years old, which is home to a vast Tesco supermarket and about twenty smaller retailers. Many of the older shops in Merrion, as in Booterstown, have been swept away in the past few decades, although one shop on the Merrion Road, Brown's newsagents, which was founded in 1908, is still trading and continues to be owned by the founding family.

Booterstown is slightly different in that its retail and hospitality outlets are all in one street, Booterstown Avenue, which is home to two of the most renowned and venerable pubs in south Co. Dublin, Gleeson's and the Old Punch Bowl. In the avenue, old shops have given way to new ones. Employment, too, has changed considerably. The old First National Building Society, once the main commercial employer in the district, is long gone but has been replaced by many newer businesses.

The two main claims to fame in both Booterstown and its continuation, Williamstown, which has almost been airbrushed out of existence in favour of Blackrock, are two renowned educational establishments. In Booterstown/ Williamstown it's Blackrock College, which has probably influenced the course of modern Irish history more than any other fee-paying second level school, while in Booterstown Avenue, St Andrew's College is equally renowned.

Booterstown has become much more of a residential suburb, especially in the area between the top of Booterstown Avenue and the Stillorgan Road, while Cross Avenue still maintains its air of exclusivity and gentility for those who can afford to live there.

As with any district in the greater Dublin area, there are people who have come to fame and prominence, including the likes of Count John McCormack, the world-famous tenor, who spent the last years of his life living in a fine house on the Rock Road at Booterstown.

Booterstown is also renowned for its marsh, a great centre for bird life, an essential part of the natural heritage of the greater Dublin area.

The two districts, Merrion and Booterstown, often offer sharp contrasts but both districts form two of the more interesting suburbs of south Co. Dublin. Just beyond Booterstown is Williamstown, so understated these days that it's often considered part of Blackrock. Originally, Williamstown village was on the Blackrock College side of the Rock Road, but around 1903 the old village was completely demolished and was reconstructed on the sea side of the Rock Road, so all the houses in present-day Williamstown date from the early twentieth century.

Hugh Oram, 2018

TIMELINE

1334

Merrion Castle is first mentioned, although it may have been built as early as 1280

***c.* 1400**

A small village exists in what is now Booterstown, but is destroyed before 1435 by Irish marauders

1686

A Catholic chapel is founded at Booterstown, making the parish one of the oldest in the country, dating back to 1616

***c.* 1706–*c.* 1771**

The Merrion brickworks are active

1779

William Scully opens his pub at the corner of Rock Road and Booterstown Avenue. A century later, in 1879, it is renamed the Old Punch Bowl

1788

Booterstown's first school is founded

1804–06

Martello tower built at Williamstown

1813

Church of the Assumption, Booterstown Avenue, is dedicated

1821

Church of Ireland parish of Booterstown is founded

1824

St Philip and St James' church in Cross Avenue is consecrated

1834

Merrion Crossing opened on the new railway line from Westland Row to Dunleary, now better known as the Merrion Gates

1835

Three railway stations open, at Merrion, Booterstown and Williamstown

1838

St Anne's Convent and orphanage run by the Sisters of Mercy opens off Booterstown Avenue

1852

St Mary's Boys' National School opens at Grotto Place, Rock Road

1860

French missionaries found what is now Blackrock College, which has a long history of academic and sporting excellence. One of the maths teachers, Éamon de Valera, later became a Taoiseach and then President of Ireland

1868

St Mary's Home and School for the Blind opens at Merrion

1869

St John's House of Rest, Anglican, opens on the Merrion Road

1883

The Merrion Seawater Baths opens on the Strand, followed the following year by a pier

1902

Leon Ó Broin is born. For many years he was secretary of the Department of Posts & Telegraphs and played a decisive role in the start of the Irish television service in 1962. He was a long-time resident of Booterstown

1927

Kevin O'Higgins, Justice and Foreign Minister, is assassinated where Cross Avenue meets Booterstown Avenue

1934

Edward Ball murders his mother, Lavena, at 23 St Helen's Road, Booterstown

1940

The temporary 'Tin Church' opens at Merrion, replaced in 1953 by Our Lady Queen of Peace church

1945

Count John McCormack dies at Glena on the Rock Road, Booterstown

1954

Frank Glennon buys Murphy's pub in Booterstown Avenue and transforms it into Gleeson's

1956

First sod turned for St Vincent's Hospital at Elm Park, Merrion, but it doesn't open until 1970

1970

An Taisce given lease to manage Booterstown Marsh

1970

Tara Towers Hotel opens on the Merrion Road

1973

St Andrew's College moves from Wellington Place, Ballsbridge, to Booterstown Avenue

1973

Merrion Hall opens on the Strand Road at Merrion, on the site of the old Merrion House

1973

The Shelter Bottle Bank opens beside the Merrion Gates

1973

Booterstown Community Centre opens

1974

St Vincent's private hospital opens beside St Vincent's public hospital. The private hospital moved to a new centre nearby in 2010

1974

The distinctive Imco laundry and dry-cleaning company's Art Deco headquarters on the Merrion Road are demolished

1981

Playwright Frank McGuinness moves to Booterstown

1984

German Embassy opens in a custom-built building at Booterstown

1987

Merrion Shopping Centre opens

1990

Japanese Embassy moves from Ailesbury Road to the Nutley Building, next door to Merrion Shopping Centre

1993

Caritas Convalescent Centre in Merrion opens

1998
First National Building Society converts to plc status and is renamed First Active

2001
Skehan House, the former headquarters of the old First National Building Society, is renamed Booterstown Hall

2004
First Active is acquired by the Ulster Bank. It traded as a separate brand until 2009, when it was fully absorbed into the Ulster Bank

2012
Merrion Inn on the Merrion Road catches fire; the rebuilt pub opens the following year

2013
Legendary poet Seamus Heaney dies; he lived at Strand Road, Merrion, although he always insisted he lived in Sandymount

2016
New traffic plan revealed for Merrion Gates; it proves controversial with local residents, and has (at the time of writing) been shelved for good.

1

HISTORY

The earliest building of note in the area was Merrion Castle, which is believed to have been built around 1280. The site on which it was built is now St Mary's Home for the Blind, just off the Merrion Road, opposite the Merrion Gates.

The first owner of Merrion Castle was Thomas Bagod, who also owned Baggotrath Castle, which once stood where Searson's pub is now located on Upper Baggot Street. Bagod gave his name to Lower and Upper Baggot Street. In the first century of its existence, Merrion Castle had a number of owners after Thomas Bagod. The castle itself was surrounded by fields, gardens and stables and the village of Merrion started to develop, to house all the people needed to work both in the castle and on its surrounding lands.

Merrion Castle and Booterstown were both mentioned in the 1488 Act that defined the boundaries of the Pale, that part of Ireland centred on the then small city of Dublin, which contained the main English-occupied areas of Ireland.

As for the name of this castle and the new village, they went under a variety of names, including Mirryyong and Meryon. It's also possible that originally the name of Merrion had been given to this whole stretch of coastline on the southern shores of Dublin Bay. The present-day name of Merrion is an anglicisation of the Irish word for seashore, *Muirbhthean*.

The original medieval castle was quite primitive and it was later replaced by a more intricate manor house. The historian F. Elrington Ball, who lived for part of his life in Booterstown and who is still regarded as the leading authority on the early history of Co. Dublin, wrote that in the sixteenth century Merrion Castle would have been a stately home surrounded by gardens, orchards and fields of corn. By the mid-eighteenth century, Merrion Castle had a neighbouring grand house, Elm Park House. At this stage, the castle itself appears to have been in ruins. In 1766, Gabriel Beranger did a drawing of the crenellated ruins of Merrion Castle, which is now in the safe custody of the National Library of Ireland.

By the end of the fourteenth century, Merrion Castle had come into the possession of the Fitzwilliam family and in subsequent centuries they held much sway over the land of south Co. Dublin, as they were the predominant landlords. The Fitzwilliam line died out in 1816 and they were succeeded by the Earls of Pembroke, to whom they were related by marriage, hence the Pembroke Estates, which controlled so much of the district.

In the eighteenth and early nineteenth centuries, Merrion became known for an entirely different reason: sea bathing. The Strand at Merrion was then ideal for this activity, and villas were built close to the shoreline; these were rented out during the summer months to visitors from Dublin. The building of a seawall at Merrion in the 1790s enabled house building in the area to expand.

By 1841, Merrion had grown into quite a substantial village, with 523 people living in a total of seventy-two houses. The arrival of the railway line from Westland Row to Dunleary in 1834 (there was even a station at Merrion that finally closed in 1935) started to make the area much more accessible for commuters who wanted to live in a pleasant seaside atmosphere and work in Dublin city centre. When the first horse trams arrived in 1872, the commuting trend was facilitated. Many of the houses and cottages that line both sides of the Merrion Road at Merrion were built in the 1850s, an indication of how popular the district had become.

The first major institutional development in Merrion came in the mid-1860s, when the Religious Sisters of Charity paid out the enormous sum of £2,000 for the ruins of Merrion Castle and its surrounding lands. In 1868, they opened St Mary's Home and School for Female Blind, followed four years later, in 1872, by St Martha's industrial school for females in the same grounds. Within a decade of its establishment, it was one of the largest industrial schools for girls in Ireland, with about 150 girls aged between 8 and 12.

On the opposite side of Merrion Road to St Mary's, another noted institution was founded the year after St Mary's had come into existence. In 1869, St John's House of Rest was established and, like St Mary's, has been there ever since. A major expansion was due to be completed in 2018.

The mid-nineteenth century saw much housing development take place beyond Merrion Road; the whole area between Merrion Road and Strand Road was developed, extending southwards from Ailesbury Road. One of the many big houses built was Ailesbury House, at the junction of Ailesbury Road and Merrion Road, which became the home of William O'Brien, of Johnston, Mooney & O'Brien bakery renown. Other notable people to have lived in Merrion included that great Dublin comic actor Jimmy O'Dea, who lived in Herbert Avenue in the 1930s. Seamus Heaney, who became a Nobel Laureate for Poetry in 1995, lived on the Strand Road in Merrion from 1976 until his death in 2013, although he always insisted, incorrectly, that he lived in Sandymount.

Developments in the twentieth century that have had a big influence on Merrion include the formation of Elm Park Golf Club in 1924; over the years since, it has expanded significantly to become one of the major golf clubs in south Co. Dublin. In 1933, the club sold some of its land at Merrion to the Sisters of Charity as a site for the new St Vincent's Hospital. Developing the hospital took an extraordinary amount of time, as it wasn't opened until 1970. Since then, many other developments have taken place at what is now St Vincent's University Hospital; the next major development due there is the building of the new National Maternity Hospital, currently located in Holles Street.

It is often said by local people that the absence of any schools in Merrion has been one of the main reasons why a community spirit has failed to develop. It's still a far more under-stated suburb than Booterstown.

However, one of the most significant developments in Merrion also took a long time to come to fruition: the Church of Our Lady, Queen of Peace, which was dedicated in 1953, replacing a temporary wooden church with a tin roof that had served the people of the area since 1940. It wasn't until the new church was opened that Merrion became a parish in its own right, something that had happened in Booterstown much earlier. Booterstown had had its own chapel since the late seventeenth century, making it one of the oldest Catholic parishes in Ireland.

There, the Church of the Assumption in Booterstown Avenue was dedicated in 1813, with an adjoining infants' school and girls' school, as well as a convent. The new parish of Booterstown had been part of a wider parish covering much of south Dublin; the earliest records of priests in Booterstown go back to 1616. The Church of Ireland church of St Philip and St James in Cross Avenue was dedicated in 1824, eleven years after the new Catholic church in Booterstown Avenue. Other 'institutions' in the area go back further, such as the Old Punch Bowl pub at the foot of Booterstown Avenue, founded in 1779.

Booterstown had started to grow earlier than Merrion. By the start of the nineteenth century, many wealthy families from Dublin were building fine houses for themselves, in Cross Avenue in particular. The old Sans Souci estate, opposite the junction of Cross Avenue and Booterstown Avenue, and long since built over, was typical of the extensive properties, with land to match, that sprung up in

Booterstown. Many smaller villas were built, too, so that by the time Samuel Lewis described Booterstown in his 1837 *A Topographical Dictionary of Ireland*, the area had 2,875 inhabitants, about ten times the number of Merrion.

The most significant event in Booterstown and its next-door neighbour, Williamstown, was undoubtedly the founding of the French College in 1860, which in due course became Blackrock College. Some of the students who studied there have had a profound influence on the development of Irish society, including Éamon de Valera, who was a student there and later became a maths teacher, to the one-time president of the College, John Charles McQuaid, who became a famous (some say notorious) Archbishop of Dublin.

Williamstown is a continuation of Booterstown, the last stop on the Rock Road before Blackrock. Williamstown started life as a bathing place and gradually housing developed along the Rock Road and between Rock Road and the railway line. By 1848, Williamstown, covering 18 hectares, had exactly ninety-four houses and a population of 575. Today, Williamstown consists of a long row of houses on the seaward side of the main Rock Road, as well as Emmet Square and Seaford Parade, between the main road and the railway line. Phoenix Terrace is the southern boundary of Booterstown, overlooking Blackrock Park.

2

ROADS AND STREETS

The main Merrion Road and Rock Road in Merrion and Booterstown can claim venerable historical antecedents.

Going back as much as 2,000 years, perhaps even further, this road started off as an ancient road, the *Slíghe Chualann*, which led from the Hill of Tara in Co. Meath, residence of the High Kings of Ireland, to *Cualann*, the ancient name for the lands that stretched as far as what is now present-day Bray, which in Irish is *Brí Cualann*.

So the Merrion and Rock Roads have long formed one of the main routes leading southwards from Dublin. Today, the Merrion Road ends at the boundary where Dublin city ended and the county begins, giving way to the Rock Road. In the eighteenth century they also connected Dublin with the emerging towns of Blackrock, Kingstown (now Dún Laoghaire) and Dalkey. During the nineteenth century, as residential developments began to spread in both Merrion and Booterstown, the road became an ever more important artery. During the nineteenth century, the traffic was entirely horse-drawn; when the first trams started to use this route in 1872, they were horse-drawn. The early 1880s saw the introduction of steam trams on the route, a short-lived innovation. Early commuters had to wait until 1896 for the tramway system to become electrified, but after the closing of the No. 8 tram route to Blackrock, Dún Laoghaire and Dalkey in 1949, public transport along the main road became exclusively buses.

Merrion, Booterstown and Williamstown also once had a number of railway stations, to complement the public transport on the main road, but these days there's only one railway station, Booterstown, an important stopping point for the DART electric trains introduced in 1984.

Many of the cottages and houses along both sides of the Merrion Road were built in the 1850s, and although they have been much updated since then, their solidity has stood them in good stead.

In Booterstown, road development was more haphazard. Booterstown Avenue was once little more than a country lane, but the building of the Church of the Assumption in the early nineteenth century, and the nearby convent and orphanage, helped consolidate the importance of the road. While Booterstown Avenue, which in its original form was known as Merrion Lane, sometimes seems straggly and unfocussed in its development, Cross Avenue is an entirely different story. It dates back two centuries, to the time when wealthy people started to build houses of great opulence for themselves. Cross Avenue was laid out as a wide thoroughfare, the last word in gentility and elegance, which it preserves to this day. It was originally called Blackrock Avenue. This avenue also performed a useful arterial function, as it linked Mount Merrion Avenue, completed in the late 1750s by the 6th Viscount Fitzwilliam, to Booterstown Avenue.

Other roads in the Booterstown area have been built over the last eighty years. St Helen's Road, which forms a loop off the main Rock Road, was built in the early 1930s. Roads in the nearby Trimleston Road, Trimleston Park area were built later, in the 1950s and '60s. Much of the housing development and roads between the grounds of St Helen's Hotel and the heart of Booterstown is even more recent, being a mere ten or twenty years old. The main Rock Road in Booterstown was known as Booterstown Strand until about a century ago.

One development mooted in 2001 was to turn the coast from Booterstown to Sandycove into Dublin's Riviera. Part of the plan included building a marine walk and a cycle path, from Sandymount to the old Blackrock Baths, via Booterstown and Williamstown. The plan remained just that; it was never progressed further. Another road plan also failed to develop. A grandiose scheme was proposed to link the Dublin Port tunnel to the M50 by building a motorway through Ringsend and Irishtown, tunnelling beneath Sandymount and Merrion Strands, exiting near Booterstown Marsh and continuing through Booterstown to join the M50 near Sandyford. Authoritative sources say that the plan has never been officially abandoned and that the plans still exist deep in the archives of Dublin City Council.

3

HISTORIC BUILDINGS AND SITES

BAYMOUNT

This small eighteenth-century house was originally on 6 hectares of land, bounded on the south by Collegnes and St Helen's. Much of its land was subsequently used for road development.

BELLEVUE

Bellevue on Cross Avenue also dates from the eighteenth century. One of its features was an elegant, oval-shaped ballroom. During the 1930s Éamon de Valera, by then Taoiseach, moved into Bellevue with his family; the house had previously been occupied by the Lee family of department store renown. Later, de Valera moved across the road to a rather ecclesiastical looking stone-built house call Herberton. In the 1970s Bellevue was converted into a private house.

BLACKROCK COLLEGE

The college has some of the finest old buildings in the area, combined with many modern additions. It began in 1860 as the French College, using Castle Dawson. Long before the French College began, Castle Dawson had been in use as a school, going back as early as the 1820s. The castle was built in 1760 by James Massey-Dawson of Aherloe, Co. Tipperary.

Subsequently, Williamstown Castle was bought in 1875. It too is an old building, dating back to 1780 when it was built by William Vavasour, after whom Williamstown was named. After Williamstown village, on the college side of Rock Road, was demolished around 1903, further work was done on Williamstown Castle in 1905, when the building was enlarged and restored. Two further purchases were of Clareville in 1899 and Willow Park in 1924. All those buildings are still standing today, except for Clareville.

The two buildings, one that houses the Junior Cycle and the Transition year, the other St Paul's Wing, opened in 2007 for the Senior Cycle, are connected by St Patrick's Corridor. Several other facilities, including community facilities, other classrooms and study specific rooms, are also linked in. Other modern facilities at the college include the computer room and the multimedia room, as well as a creative arts and digital learning centre. The Quad is a large green area, surrounded by St Paul's School senior wing, the chapel, St Mary's Corridor and the Jubilee Hall. Other facilities at the college include the new sports hall, opened in 2012.

BOOTERSTOWN CASTLE

Booterstown Castle, which is next door to Booterstown House, is far older, having been built in about 1449 to defend the then small village, which had already been wiped out in the early fifteenth century. The castle is incorporated into the structure of an eighteenth-century house. This new house was added to the old castle in a very clever way and a new façade was created by making large windows in the thick walls of the castle. Originally, the house with castle continued to be called Booterstown Castle, but it was later renamed St Mary's.

BOOTERSTOWN HOUSE

Originally a fairly small house, Booterstown house was built around 1760, facing the wide lane that led to Rosemount and the back entrance to St Helen's. Despite the many subsequent additions to the house, it remained just one room deep. A feature of the house is the spacious upstairs drawing room, which overlooks the garden. At the foot of the garden is an unusual feature, a short spiral staircase leading to a culverted stream. Perhaps the most noted occupant of Booterstown House over the years was Francis Elrington Ball, whose book *A History of County Dublin* was published in 1903 and remains the most authoritative work on the early history of the county.

CASTLE DAWSON

Built in 1762, this became the first home of the French Fathers, who started the predecessor of Blackrock College. The house still has its mid-eighteenth-century features, including fine plasterwork ceilings and cornices and the original doors and staircases. In the 1870s, a covered gallery was added to link the house to the chapel and to St Patrick's Hall. The chapel was completed in 1868 and these new buildings, originating in the old house, form a nearly perfect quadrangle.

At the same time that these extensions were being added, the original Williamstown Castle was bought and a large dining hall built. The original castle was two storeys over a basement; it even had a viewing tower on the roof. The castle was substantially enlarged in 1905 and 1906, including the addition of three storeys over basement wings. In more recent times Williamstown Castle has been used to accommodate boarders at Blackrock College. Unfortunately, another eighteenth-century building in the grounds of Blackrock College, Clareville, didn't survive.

CHERBURY

This was another fine eighteenth-century villa built on the Fitzwilliam estate, just off the top end of Booterstown Avenue. This villa was substantially extended to produce a long frontage of twelve windows, overlooking the gardens. During the later eighteenth century, the villa was home to Sir Samuel Bradstreet, a noted lawyer and Dublin MP. After the death of his widow in 1802, the house was advertised as being for rent. It was described as having thirteen rooms and six formal gardens, some used for fruit growing, and a miniaturised parkland. The house was demolished during the 1970s to make way for the vast Cherbury Court apartment complex, which still occupies the site today.

CHESTERFIELD

Chesterfield, a secluded house set back from Cross Avenue, dates from the early nineteenth century, when Cross Avenue as it is known today was substantially developed. The large house now bears little resemblance to its original appearance.

COLLEGNES

This eighteenth-century villa just off Booterstown Avenue is now the site of St Andrew's College. The original house was very plain, just three windows wide, but it was later enlarged with extra rooms at each end and a new portico.

DAWSON COURT

This three-storey Georgian house was a dower house of Castle Dawson, which was in the grounds of Blackrock College. Dawson Court was close to Mount Merrion Avenue and had striking Georgian features both inside and outside. The house was sold in 1971 but subsequently vandalised; sadly the house was so badly damaged that it had to be demolished.

ELM PARK GREEN

This huge office development, which covers 7 hectares just off the Merrion Road, has mainly office space, but it also includes residential units. Close by is a residential centre for the elderly. Close to the Merrion Road, the Seamark Building is a very visible sign of this huge mixed-use campus, which many local residents find visually intrusive.

GLENA

This 1888 house on the Rock Road at Booterstown was the last home of Count John McCormack, the world-famous tenor, who died here in 1945. It's a villa-type house, one storey over basement, with its principal rooms giving fine sea

views over Dublin Bay. Its most striking feature is a corner tower, with large window, topped by a cone-shaped roof. Its five reception rooms include an oratory-style annexe to the drawing room, complete with magnificent stained-glass windows. The house was named after its builder, a man called Glennan. In early 2018 the house was up for sale with an asking price of €2.5 million.

GLENVAR

One of the most distinctive-looking houses on Cross Avenue, Glenvar was built in 1856 and had many Oriental-looking features, such as bracketed eves.

IMCO WORKS

The old Imco works on the Merrion Road were one of the most striking architectural features of Booterstown. The Imco cleaning and dyeing company had been founded by the Spiro family in 1927 and the following decade they decided to build a new headquarters on the Merrion Road. The original building, made from reinforced concrete, was unremarkable, but subsequently a dramatic stair tower, designed in the modern international style of the time, turned the Imco building into an icon for the area. The exterior of the tower featured the company name 'Imco' and a large clock.

But by the 1960s, the idea of a centralised dry-cleaning plant had become obsolete as cleaning was moved to individual shops. Imco sold its Merrion Road works in 1974, which were subsequently demolished. The Imco factory was replaced by a nondescript office block, still there today.

LANDAFF TERRACE, MERRION

Landaff Terrace was built in Victorian times; it abuts the Tara Towers Hotel on the main road at Merrion. The terrace of houses had got into a rundown state, but in 2016 a US company, the Starwood Capital Group, bought the vast residential and office development at Elm Park; included in its purchase were the houses at Landaff Terrace. It then spent a vast but undisclosed amount of money on a total refurbishment of the houses. Once the double-fronted houses were restored and fitted with many new extras, they were put on the market in early 2018.

The townhouses have two, three and four bedrooms and range from 90 to 185 square metres. The selling price of the houses was substantial, ranging from €665,000 to €920,000. In all the media publicity for the development, not a word was devoted to the previous occupiers of the terrace and what had happened to them.

MARTELLO TOWER

Close to the railway line at Williamstown and near the green space widely used for circus performances is the Martello tower, built between 1804 and 1806. The threat of a Napoleonic invasion of Ireland, which never materialised, prompted the building of many Martello towers in Ireland, mostly, but not entirely, along the east coast.

The one at Williamstown is one of sixteen built between Sandymount and Bray.

Since the Martello tower had been built on the foreshore, it was liable to flooding during high tides. The coming of the railway in 1834, between Westland Row and Dun Leary, meant that ever since the tower has been landlocked. In 2013, Dún Laoghaire-Rathdown county council agreed to spend €100,000 on renovations for the tower, so that it could be used for exhibitions and other civic events.

MCCABE'S VILLAS

McCabe's Villas in Booterstown, just off Rosemount Terrace, which itself is off Booterstown Avenue, were built in the early 1930s on land sold by a local parishioner. A total of seventy houses were built and the seventy families who moved into them consisted of 250 people. Some local sources claim that the villas were named after the parishioner who had owned the land, while others say that they were named after a local councillor who owned what was McCabe's pub, at the foot of Booterstown Avenue, on the opposite side of the road to the Old Punch Bowl.

MERRION CASTLE

This elaborate, elongated building dates back to the eighteenth century. It has been owned by the Sisters of Charity since 1866, when they bought the land here to set up St Mary's Blind Asylum. The Sisters built a convent, a school and a large granite chapel onto the house.

The Blind Asylum still continues its work on the same site, which has seen many modifications in recent years.

The original Merrion Castle had been built in the early fourteenth century on a site that now houses St Mary's Blind Asylum. From the sixteenth to the early eighteenth century, Merrion Castle was the seat of the Fitzwilliam family. It was one of the largest private dwellings in the Dublin area. After they left, to go and live in Mount Merrion House, the castle fell into ruin and was demolished in 1780. However, Samuel Lewis's *A Topographical Dictionary of Ireland* (1837), said that some ivy-covered ruins of the castle still existed at that date.

MERRION GRAVEYARD

Between Tara Towers Hotel and the Applegreen service station on the main road at Merrion is the former Merrion graveyard, which was in use from the early fourteenth century up until 1866. Since 1978 it has been a public park, maintained by Dublin City Council. It covers an area of 1,730 square metres.

The graveyard once had a church, built in the fourteenth century by John Cruise of nearby Merrion Castle, but today there are no remains left of that ancient church.

In November 1807, several ships left Dublin and Kingstown with soldiers bound for the Napoleonic wars. One of them was the *Prince of Wales*, a sloop weighing 103 tons. The weather was violently stormy and the ship was blown onto rocks at Blackrock. All 120 soldiers, who were below decks, were drowned, but Captain Robert Jones, two women with children, who were members of his family, nine

seamen and two soldiers escaped in a single lifeboat. Later, the captain was accused of murder, but since there were no witnesses the case was dismissed.

The bodies of the 120 soldiers who died were buried in the Merrion graveyard and their tombstone can still be seen today. The same night that the *Prince of Wales* went down, another ship, the *Rochdale*, sank off the south Dublin coast with the loss of 265 lives. Most of the bodies from that disaster were buried in Monkstown, rather than Merrion.

MULCAIRE

A large Victorian house was built on land that adjoins what is now Willow Park; Mulcaire lasted until 1971, when it was sold and then demolished to make way for the new headquarters of the old First National Building Society.

ST ANDREW'S COLLEGE

This college has a proud history going back to 1894, when it was founded on St Stephen's Green. It later moved to Wellington Place in Ballsbridge, in 1937. Then, thirty-six years later, the new school in Booterstown Avenue was opened. The site was occupied by a derelict house, Collegnes, which has been used as a school by the Sisters of Mercy, then subsequently as a commercial storehouse. The old house was demolished and the first sod on the new site was turned on 28 November 1971. The new school buildings were placed at the southern end of the site, surrounded by trees, while the northern end was earmarked for playing fields. The purchase of another house on Booterstown Avenue, No. 55, and the acquisition of land from the Convent of Mercy opened alternative access to the college. The move into the brand new school came during the Christmas vacation, 1972.

SANS SOUCI

The name of Sans Souci Park, just off Booterstown Avenue and opposite Cross Avenue, is all that remains of a once renowned big house in the area. It was built around 1760 by the Earl of Lanesborough and was a small, double-fronted house, to which a large wing was added forty years later.

This wing provided a new entrance to the house and on either side of the new hallway there were two substantial reception rooms. At the back of the house, many outbuildings included stables and a diary. This extension to the house was carried out at the start of the nineteenth century for the then new resident, William Digges La Touche, whose Huguenot family had made a fortune in banking during the eighteenth century. His main town residence was in St Stephen's Green, while Sans Souci became his country residence, noted for its extensive gardens. Having been semi-derelict for a number of years, Sans Souci was demolished in 1948.

ST HELEN'S

Now a hotel, St Helen's was once the finest house in Booterstown, if not the country. The house was started in 1754, built for Thomas Cooley, a Dublin barrister and MP. It later belonged to Robert Alexander, one of the early patrons of the Church of Ireland's church of St Philip and St James, Cross Avenue, opened in 1824. In the late nineteenth century the house was greatly enlarged by Viscount Lord Henry Gough, who had spent much of his career in service with the British Army. In 1898, Sir John Nutting, a wealthy railway director, added more flourishes by facing the brick façade with Portland stone. The stone façade and balustrade was added to unify the eighteenth- and nineteenth-century parts of the house.

Nutting also carried out a complete reordering of the interior, in a very lavish style, making extensive use of Italian marble and decorative plasterwork. The great ballroom, with its fluted columns and gallery, had its organ reinstated. However, during this big extension of St Helen's, the nineteenth-century terraced gardens remained untouched.

In 1925, St Helen's was bought by the Christian Brothers as their provincial residence and novitiate and they stayed there until 1988. One of the changes was to turn the ballroom, with its organ, into a chapel. During the 1920s, surplus land from the St Helen's estate was sold so that St Helen's Road in Booterstown could be built. Two large tracts of land fronting the Stillorgan Road were sold to facilitate the building of two schools, Coláiste Eoin and Coláiste Íosagáin. When what remained of the St Helen's estate was sold to a property developer in 1988, local residents feared that the big house would go the way of Frascati House in Blackrock, which had been demolished. Fortunately, the house was saved and eventually turned into a luxury hotel, while many apartments were built on the periphery of the estate.

SUMMERVILLE

This fine Victorian house, built around 1858, stands at the corner of Cross Avenue and Booterstown Avenue. The ground-floor windows and the entrance have fine ironwork canopies and on the roof there's a fancy ironwork weathervane.

TRIMLESTON HOUSE

Dating back to the Regency period of the early nineteenth century, this five-bay house with granite porch and a stucco embellished façade was substantially remodelled in 1870. However, it failed to survive the twentieth century, having been demolished in 1974. All that remains today is the stone-built gate lodge at the corner of Trimleston Avenue and the Merrion Road.

WILLOW PARK

The lands of Willow Park were leased from Lord Fitzwilliam by John Grainger in 1751, but it wasn't until later in the 1760s that Christopher Deery, a public notary, built a house there. Willow Park was a substantial three-storey house, which was further extended in the nineteenth century. Many prominent families lived there, including James Ferrier, of Ferrier Pollock, the clothing wholesaler, in the early nineteenth century, and the Bewleys, who lived there from 1859 until 1924.

In 1925, the house was purchased by Blackrock College for use as its preparatory school, still in existence today. Just after the purchase, the ball-topped stone piers of the entrance gate were put in place; they had come from the Mount Merrion estate.

4

CRIME

THE BALL MURDER

When Edward Ball murdered his mother at St Helen's Road in Booterstown in 1936, it soon became one of the most notorious murders in Ireland of the twentieth century.

Edward Ball had been born at 40 Upper Fitzwilliam Street, Dublin, in 1916. He went to Shrewsbury School in England, but after he left there in 1934 he had difficulties settling into life back in Dublin and was unable to find a job. He took on several unpaid, walk-on parts at the Gate Theatre, Dublin.

Ball's parents had split up in 1927; his father was Charles Ball, a Dublin medical doctor who died in 1957, while his mother, Lavena, or Vena, had a foul temper and may have been mentally deranged. But she was a woman of independent means, with £12,000 in securities. She lived at 23 St Helen's Road, Booterstown, and Edward lived mainly with her there.

On 17 February 1936, Edward had a big disagreement with his mother, when she refused to give him £60 to go on a foreign tour with the Gate Theatre Company. He then killed her with a hatchet, moved her body by car to Corbawn Lane in Shankill, south Co. Dublin, and dumped the corpse in the sea. It was never recovered.

In May of that year, at the end of a six-day trial, Edward Ball was found guilty of his mother's murder, but insane. He spent fourteen years' incarcerated in what was then the Central Criminal Lunatic Asylum in Dundrum, where he received regular visits from Dorothy Macardle, a writer and friend and confidante of Éamon de Valera, by then Taoiseach. Dorothy secured various privileges in the asylum for Ball.

After his release in 1950, Ball went to Paris and admitted his guilt freely to his friend Richard Cobb, who had been a schoolmate at Shrewsbury School. Cobb was an historian and the details of the Ball murder formed his 1985 book, *A Classical Education*. Later, Ball went to England, where he obtained employment with the Automobile Association in London. He died in 1987.

In 1994, RTÉ screened a TV series presented by Cathal O'Shannon called *Thou Shalt Not Kill*, about thirteen infamous Irish murder cases. Naturally, the Ball murder was included. A friend of O'Shannon's, Gerry Downey, a Dublin barber, took part in the episode about the Ball murder. Years after the murder, Gerry Downey's family had a holiday caravan at Corbawn Lane in Shankill, and one night Gerry, then a young lad, woke up in a panic, thinking he had been seeing ghosts related to the Ball murder. He duly recounted the story in the TV series.

THE ASSASSINATION OF KEVIN O'HIGGINS

The murder of government minister Kevin O'Higgins in Booterstown Avenue in 1927 was one of the most notorious political assassinations in Ireland during the twentieth century.

During the civil war in Ireland, between 1922 and 1923, O'Higgins had made many enemies on the republican side, which opposed the 1922 Treaty. He had been responsible for many republicans being executed. By 1927, O'Higgins had become an important minister in the pro-Treaty government led by W.T. Cosgrave. O'Higgins was not only vice-president of the executive council, equivalent today to the post of Tanaiste, but he was also Minister for Justice and Minister for External Affairs.

On the morning of Sunday, 10 July 1927, O'Higgins had gone for his usual swim in Blackrock. His personal guard stayed in Blackrock to get some cigarettes and, sensing no danger, had returned to the O'Higgins' home at Dunamase in Cross Avenue.

Later that morning, O'Higgins set out to walk the short distance to Mass in the Church of the Assumption in Booterstown Avenue. Three gunmen were waiting in a car on Booterstown Avenue, near where Booterstown Park is now located.

Seeing the gunmen running from the car towards him, O'Higgins ran to take cover in the grounds of Sans Souci, where Sans Souci Park is now located. The gate to Sans Souci was open but before he could reach it, O'Higgins fell to the ground under a hail of bullets. As he lay dying on the road, the gunmen fired more bullets into him. Later, a relative of the gunman revealed that, as he lay dying, O'Higgins forgave his killers the terrible deed they had done.

An ambulance arrived from St Vincent's Hospital, then on St Stephen's Green, but O'Higgins refused to go to hospital. A bed was made up for him in the dining room of his house, Dunamase, but he died some hours later, at 5 p.m. that evening. The funeral in St Andrew's church, Westland Row, was a momentous occasion, with vast crowds of people lining the city streets. The funeral cortege stretched for over 5km.

In 1987, on the sixtieth anniversary of her father's murder, one of his two daughters, Una O'Higgins O'Malley, a peace activist, arranged a Mass of Reconciliation at the church in Booterstown Avenue. Some months before, the names of the three men who carried out the murder were revealed: Tim Coughlan, Archie Doyle and Bill Gannon. It was said that the three men had been on their way to a football match when they realised how easy it would be to assassinate Kevin O'Higgins.

No one was ever convicted of the murder. Someone who was questioned and charged, but later released, was Sean MacBride, who had been the chief of staff of the Old IRA and who later became a government minister himself. He was living in Booterstown at the time and it was claimed that he had been involved in the crime.

5

WELL-KNOWN RESIDENTS

F. ELRINGTON BALL

Noted historian Francis Elrington Ball lived for some of his life at Booterstown House in Booterstown Avenue. Born in 1863, he wrote extensively about legal history, but his seminal work is the history of Co. Dublin from earliest times to the end of the eighteenth century. This has long been regarded as the most definitive work on the early history of Co. Dublin. He died in 1928.

BOOTERSTOWN PRIESTS

Over the years, the Booterstown parish has seen many parish priests. Initially the area was part of a much wider parish, embracing Donnybrook, Dundrum and Booterstown. The first parish priest was Revd James Cahill, who served from 1616 until 1650. In more recent times, after Booterstown became a separate parish, the Very Revd Edward Dunne was the first parish priest, from 1922 to 1927. He was followed by the Very Revd James Breen, who remained in Booterstown until 1939. Father Paddy Flanagan then became parish priest, from 1939 until 1956, after which, until 1964, the parish priest was Patrick Scannell, followed by Cecil Barrett, from 1964 until 1976. From then until 1993 Jerome Curtin was the parish priest, while from 1993 until 2012 the parish was under Seamus Conway, who is now pastor emeritus. The present parish priest in Gerry Kane. All the previous parish priests are commemorated by plaques in the Church of the Assumption just off Booterstown Avenue.

MICHAEL BOWLES

Michael Bowles started his career in advertising in 1964 and after working with two Dublin advertising agencies he moved to London. He later returned to Dublin and in 1969 joined Hunter Advertising, a start-up agency that soon became very successful. He also lectured on media at the Rathmines College of Commerce. In 1976 he set up The Media Bureau, the first media planning and buying agency in Ireland, whose advent started the process of unravelling the traditional full-service advertising agency in Ireland. The company was based in the Nutley Building beside the Merrion Shopping Centre. The Media Bureau worked with many national and international clients, as well as with UK and other international ad agencies that didn't have any representation in Ireland. In 2000, Michael sold the company to his colleagues and became a spectator in the media business, struggling, in his own words, to become an unsuccessful script and short story writer.

MAZIERE BRADY

Maziere Brady (1796–1871) was born at Willow Park in Booterstown, which his family owned. He was called to the Bar in 1819 and became a King's Counsel in 1835. In 1846 he was made Lord Chancellor of Ireland and remained in that post for twenty years, without any particular distinction. His appointment had ended the practice, since the Act of Union in 1800, of appointing English lawyers to the post. In politics he was liberal and had supported Catholic emancipation. He was made a baronet in 1866.

HUGH CARLETON, 1ST VISCOUNT CARLETON

Hugh Carleton (1739–1826) was born in Cork and became a noted politician and judge. He was an MP in the Irish House of Commons in the 1770s and early 1880s. As a politician he wasn't very successful, as everyone complained they couldn't hear him, but this shortcoming didn't prevent him becoming a successful judge, even though his appearance was sombre and he was a notorious hypochondriac, despite enjoying good health. He was raised to the peerage in 1789. Married twice, he lived at Willow Park in Booterstown for many years, as well as in Dublin, while he spent the last years of his life in London.

KENNY CARROLL

Born at Booterstown in 1983, Kenny Carroll went on to become an outstanding cricketer, making his debut with Ireland's senior cricket team in 2006 when he played in the European Championships that year. As a right-handed batsman and a right arm leg break bowler, he has played for Ireland in many other international tournaments, including hockey, winning several caps.

HARRY CLIFTON

Harry Clifton, a noted poet, has long lived at Cross Avenue, Booterstown. Born in Dublin in 1952, he was educated at Blackrock College and then UCD. A renowned traveller over the years, he worked first as a teacher of English in Africa, then as an aid administrator in Thailand for eight years, from 1980 to 1988, before returning home to teach. He has a substantial reputation for his poetry, which has a sardonic edge and addresses many global social issues. He's not only a professor of poetry, but he also teaches at UCD. Clifton was in college with Frank McGuinness; they later met on Cross Avenue and have been friends for well over forty years.

ÉAMON DE VALERA

Éamon de Valera had close connections with Booterstown since he was a teenager, when he won a scholarship to Blackrock College. He studied there between 1898 and 1900, but he continued his connection with the Williamstown campus until 1903, when he did his university studies with the old Royal University of Ireland. At the time he was recorded as living in Williamstown Avenue.

In 1908 he moved lodgings to Merrion, when he moved to Merrion View Avenue, just beside the present-day Merrion Shopping Centre. After graduating he continued his connection with the Booterstown area by returning to Blackrock College to teach mathematics there, while he also taught in Our Lady of Mercy teacher training college at Carysfort, not far from Blackrock College. After de Valera married Sinéad Flanagan, a Balbriggan-born schoolteacher, in 1910, they lived briefly at Vernon Terrace in Booterstown.

Later, de Valera and his wife lived at Herberton on Cross Avenue, Booterstown, next door to Chesterfield. By the 1930s they had seven children, one of whom, Brian, was tragically killed in a riding accident in the Phoenix Park. Between 1933 and 1940 the family lived at Bellevue, one of the oldest houses on Cross Avenue, which dated from the mid-eighteenth century. It was at Bellevue that much of the work was done on drafting the 1937 constitution, which, among many other changes, altered the title of de Valera's job from head of the executive council to Taoiseach.

In the 1930s, when he was head of government, he was frequently sighted walking along the Strand Road at Merrion. On these walks he was always accompanied by his armed guard, as he was at high risk of being assassinated by the IRA, while his official car drove alongside him.

His first spell as head of government lasted for fifteen years, until 1947, but later he returned to that job, remaining Taoiseach until 1959, when he became President of Ireland. He died in 1975, aged 92.

DAVE DOWNES

During the 1970s, Dave Downes was the manager of the old bottle recycling centre near the Merrion Gates, about which he has many tales. He has had a very varied career, including in the probation service and running the Irish Youth Foundation. Having been an avid collector of books for many years, he set up Dublin Book Browsers in 1996, buying and selling old books, as well as other materials, such as postcards and posters. He runs the business from his home in Stillorgan.

WILLIAM DOWNES

William Downes (1751–1826) was one of the leading Irish judges of his time and also Lord Chief Justice. Although he was stern and intimidating and never laughed, he was respected for his integrity. He was also one of the few judges that Daniel O'Connell could not intimidate. After he retired in 1822, he was elevated to the peerage, becoming the first Baron Downes. During his lifetime he lived for many years in Booterstown. When he died he was buried at St Anne's church in Dawson Street, Dublin, next to his inseparable friend of many years, William Chamberlain.

FATHER PADDY FLANAGAN

Father Flanagan was an often controversial cleric who was parish priest of Booterstown from 1939 until 1956; he was also heavily involved in the construction of the new church on the Merrion Road, Our Lady Queen of Peace, which was dedicated in 1953. Merrion became a parish in its own right in 1964.

Born in Dublin in 1883, Fr Flanagan was a curate at Ringsend from 1909 to 1918 and also put his strongly nationalistic views into practice. A couple of years after being appointed to Ringsend, he set up the Fianna Phadraig, which was similar to the Fianna Éireann. He taught the young men who joined his organisation a very nationalistic version of Irish history and also equipped them with rifles. During the 1916 Easter Rising, he was briefly jailed. Then, in 1919, he was appointed curate at Aughrim Street, a position he held for twenty years, until he moved to Booterstown.

When the new church was being built on the Merrion Road, Fr Flanagan was given instructions from Archbishop John Charles McQuaid that he was to get a round tower

built beside the church. Father Flanagan didn't approve of this at all, but he had no option but to go along with higher orders on the matter. A former Taoiseach, the late Liam Cosgrave, used to say that some people in the parish called the round tower 'Flanagan's Folly'. Father Flanagan died in 1956, aged 73.

MAI GELDOF

Mai Geldof, the aunt of singer and humanitarian activist Bob Geldof, lived for many years in a Victorian double-fronted villa on Strand Road at Merrion. The house had previously been home to her father, Zenon Geldof, who came from Ypres in Belgium to work in Dublin as a master chef. Mai worked as a dressmaker in Wicklow Street, in Dublin's city centre, but she had an active social life and she saw some notable events as they happened, such as the Nazi invasion of Austria just before the Second World War. She was also a champion fisherwoman and often practised her fishing skills in the West of Ireland. When she was in her 70s, she learnt to drive. She was an altogether remarkable woman.

After her death at the age of 105 in 2015, her house on the Strand Road was put on the market for €1.5 million.

MARY HANAFIN

Born in Thurles, Co. Tipperary, in 1959, Mary Hanafin has had a long connection with politics; her late father, Des Hanafin, was a well-known senator. After Mary graduated, she worked as a secondary level teacher of Irish and history at the Dominican College in Sion Hill, so she has had a long connection with the Booterstown area. In 1985 she married Eamon Leahy, a senior counsel, who tragically died in 2003, aged 46.

Mary has also had a long career as a Fianna Fáil politician, being first elected to the Dáil in 1997. Between 2000 and 2011 she held various Ministerial portfolios, while she was also government chief whip from 2002 to 2004. Often controversial, she returned to politics, but at local level, when in 2014 she became a local councillor for the Blackrock area.

SEAMUS HEANEY

Seamus Heaney was not only one of the most important poets that Ireland produced in the twentieth century, but one of the world's leading poets. Born in Co. Derry in 1939, he studied at Queen's University before moved south to teach at Carysfort Training College in Blackrock. Later in his career, he taught at such prestigious academic venues as Harvard and Oxford.

Early in his time in the South, he lived in a remote cottage in Co. Wicklow, but for the last thirty years of his life he and his family lived on the Strand Road. He used to say he lived in Sandymount, but his house was in fact in Merrion. His wife Marie is one of the remarkable six Devlin sisters, from Ardboe in Co. Tyrone, close to Lough Neagh. She had three children with Seamus.

He was awarded the greatest accolade of his career in 1995 when he was awarded the Nobel Prize for Literature. Altogether, he wrote over twenty volumes of poetry and criticism, as well as editing several anthologies. His poetry often reflected day-to-day experiences, while he was also influenced by motifs from history, going right back to prehistoric times. One of the nicknames given him was 'Famous Seamus'.

In August 2013, he had a fall while coming out of a restaurant; he was rushed to hospital, but never recovered. His last text message to his wife, from his hospital bed, minutes before he died, was 'Noli Timere' (do not be afraid).

MAUREEN HURLEY

A long-time resident of Merrion, living in Merrion Court, Maureen Hurley had a remarkable musical talent. In the 1950s and '60s, photographs of her playing her harp were often used by the old Bord Fáilte on posters in Europe and North America. She was also the first Irish harpist to appear on Russian television. In the late 1950s she joined the BBC's music department in London, and when Telefís Éireann started in 1962, she came home to join the new television service as its first production assistant. But she continued to make many appearances as a concert harpist.

Her father, Seán, who came from Durrus in west Cork, had an even more remarkable career. From 1905 until 1915 he lived in China, one of the first Irishmen to visit that country and the first Irishman to get a Chinese passport. He helped train activists loyal to Sun Yat-Sen, founding father of the Republic of China and known as the father of the nation in China, who had brought about the collapse of the Qing dynasty in 1911.

As for Maureen herself, in later life her health deteriorated and she died in St Vincent's Hospital in June 2011, aged 85.

JOHNNY ON THE ROCK ROAD

Although he was a well-known character in Booterstown during the late 1970s and early 1980s, Johnny wasn't exactly a resident as he had no permanent home of his own. He was a scruffy-looking character with a long matted beard, who used to spend his time walking back and forth along the Rock Road, carrying a long timber pole. Whether he thought he was a latter-day Messiah, no one knew, but like all itinerant characters he eventually faded from view and has been long forgotten. No one was quite sure of his name, although some called him Johnny and others called him, inaccurately, Johnny Forty Coats, who was in fact another itinerant character in the Dublin of that era.

VAL JOYCE

For long a radio presenter on RTÉ, noted for his late-night shows, Val Joyce lived for many years in Booterstown. His wife Vera died in 2016. Val worked for over fifty years as a radio presenter on RTÉ, having begun his career with sponsored programmes in the 1950s. He often appeared on the old Irish Hospitals' Sweepstakes programme, recorded in studios at the old Red House, opposite the RDS Main Hall; the building is now derelict. In the 1960s he also did the voiceovers for many television commercials, after the start of Telefís Éirean.

Val suffered a terminal blow to his career when, in 2006, RTÉ decided not to continue his late-night show, Late Date, on Radio 1. His new boss, Ana Leddy, who axed the show, said that Val would continue to broadcast for Radio 1, but that never happened.

CATHERINE KILBRIDE

Catherine, who has lived on the Merrion Road in Merrion for many years, has had a long career in teaching, since she graduated from UCD. She spent a few years as PA to the French-speaking Belgian ambassador, then a few more years working as a teacher in Zambia. She inherited her love of music from her mother, a gifted musician, and Catherine became a member of the Guinness Choir.

During the 1980s she was principal of Pembroke School in Pembroke Road, Ballsbridge, often known as 'Miss Meredith's School'. She also enjoyed several years as a guest lecturer at UCD. When she was appointed Director of Education at the Marketing Institute, her duties included the commissioning and editing of material to make the entire four-year course available by distance learning.

This experience, together with her professional qualification as a translator, led to her current freelance career as a copy-editor, researcher, proofreader and translator. She co-authored, with Dr Deirdre Raftery, two education-related books, one in 2007, the other in 2009. More recently she has published her first novel, *Friend or Lover?*, which sets Jane Austen's Emma in twenty-first century Dublin.

CHARLES LYSAGHT

A noted barrister and author, Charles Lysaght is also noted for the obituaries he has written, especially for the *Sunday Independent* and *The Times*. Born in Dublin in 1941, he has been a resident of Strand Road, Merrion, for virtually his whole life and is a noted authority on the area's history. Charles is resolute about the fact that he has always lived in Merrion and most certainly not in Sandymount. He says that traditionally, Merrion began at the Martello tower, but in recent years places like the upper part of Strand Road, Sydney Parade and St Alban's Park, although in Merrion, are now inaccurately described by estate agents and other as being in Sandymount.

His third level education was at UCD and he went on to become president of the Cambridge Union in 1964. Between 1967 and 1970 he lectured on law in London while practising at the Bar. In 1970 he returned home and during the following decade was a legal adviser to what is now the Department of Foreign Affairs and Trade. From there he went on to work for such bodies as the Irish Law Reform Commission and the National Archives. In sporting terms, he has always been a keen cricketer and once broke his arm whilst playing cricket in his 50s.

RICHARD ROBERT MADDEN

Richard Madden, who was born in Dublin in 1798, spent much of his life working in foreign posts, living and working in places as widely separated as Havana, Lisbon and Western Australia. Later in life, when he had returned to Ireland, he became a noted historian. His most prominent work, published in seven volumes between 1842 and 1846, chronicled the life and times of the United Irishmen. He lived for many years at what was then 3 Vernon Terrace, but is now 3 Booterstown Avenue, where a plaque to him can be found. Dr Madden died there on 5 February 1886, aged 88. It's a fine end of terrace house, built in red brick in the early nineteenth century, next door to the Old Punch Bowl pub.

EÓIN MACNEILL

Eóin MacNeill was one of the most prominent figures in Irish politics in the early twentieth century, born in Glenarm, Co. Antrim, in 1867.

By turn he was an Irish scholar, an Irish language enthusiast and a Sinn Féin politician. He was a key figure in the Gaelic revival at the start of the twentieth century and a co-founder of the Gaelic League. In 1913 he formed the Irish Volunteers and became its chief of staff, although he played no part in the 1916 Easter Rising or its planning, which was done by members of the Irish Republican Brotherhood. He became famous for advising people at the last minute not to take part in the Rising. When the first Dáil was set up in 1919, he was elected as a member of Sinn Féin and when the first government of the Irish Free State was set up in 1922, MacNeill became Minister for Education.

He also had a long academic career, having been made professor of early Irish history at UCD in 1908. Later in life he became president of the Royal Society of Antiquaries of Ireland, from 1937 to 1940, and then from 1940 until 1943, president of the Royal Irish Academy. He was also chairman of the Irish Manuscripts Commission as well as writing a number of books on Irish history. He died in 1945, aged 78.

For many years he lived at South Hill Avenue, Booterstown. One of his grandsons is the barrister and former government minister, Michael McDowell.

FRANK MCGUINNESS

Frank McGuinness, a well-known writer, was born in Buncrana, Co. Donegal, in 1953. He first came to prominence with his play *The Factory Girls*, while he made his reputation as a playwright with his play set during the First World War, *Observe the Sons of Ulster Marching Towards the Somme*. He has also adapted many classics as plays, and produced four collections of poetry. He has also written opera libretti as well as TV and film scripts and in 2013, his first novel, *Arimathea*, was published. Since 2007 this very versatile writer has been Professor of Creative Writing at UCD.

He moved to his present house in Booterstown in 1981; the house is at the intersection of Booterstown Avenue and Cross Avenue, in what he calls a holy triangle that also encompasses Mount Merrion Avenue. He lives there with his partner, Phillip. But McGuinness's acquaintance with Booterstown goes back much further; he came to Dublin when he was 18 and stayed in Willow Park, enjoying his first pint in Gleeson's on Booterstown Avenue.

MAURICE NELIGAN

Born in Booterstown in 1937, Maurice Neligan was educated at nearby Blackrock College and then studied medicine at UCD. He became a heart surgeon and during his career performed around 15,000 heart operations. He performed a number of firsts in Irish surgery and became known as Ireland's answer to Dr Christian Barnard, who had performed the world's first heart transplant. In 1974, Neligan performed the first open heart surgery to correct heart defects and in 1984 carried out Ireland's first heart transplant. He was also a co-founder of the Blackrock Clinic. After he retired from his medical career, he turned to writing and wrote a weekly column on health matters for *The Irish Times*, in which he was a fierce critic of government health policy.

Married to Pat, a fellow doctor, they had seven children, but tragedy struck in 2007 when their daughter Sara was murdered. The family received 12,000 letters of sympathy from the public. When Maurice Neligan died in 2010, the then leader of Fine Gael, Enda Kenny, described him as the first superstar of Irish medicine.

ANITA NOTARO

A well-known television producer who worked for RTÉ for many years, working on the television coverage of many events and programmes such as the Eurovision Song Contest and the Fair City series, Anita Notaro turned to writing in later life. She wrote half a dozen best-selling novels, all against the background of poor health, having battled against breast cancer in 2005– the year after she married Gerry McGuinness in Co. Wicklow. She gave up her eighteen-year-long television career to become a writer and did most of her writing in Co. Wicklow. Sadly, a diagnosis of front temporal dementia in 2011 ended her literary career. She died on 26 November 2014. Anita and her husband had a close connection with Merrion as they lived on the Merrion Road in Merrion.

LEON Ó BROIN

Leon Ó Broin was a civil servant who did more than anyone else in the 1950s to push for the development of an Irish television service.

Born in Dublin in 1902, he was imprisoned in 1921 and 1922, later joining the Free State Army as a non-combatant. In 1924 he was made the first administrative officer appointed by the new civil service; from then until 1948 he worked mainly in the Department of Finance. Then, in 1948, he was made Secretary of the Department of Finance, a role he held until 1967. There, he set up a committee to look at the merits of establishing an Irish television service and he is considered to have done more than anyone else during the earlier part of the 1950s to press for the start of Telefís Éireann, now RTÉ.

Apart from his day job as a top civil servant, Ó Broin was also a well-regarded writer, in both English and Irish. He wrote a number of books in Irish, three plays in Irish and he also did translations into Irish of such books as *The War of the Worlds* by H.G. Wells. Leon Ó Broin died in 1990.

One of his children became equally well-known, but in an entirely different career. Éimear O'Broin, born in 1927, was brought up in the family home in Booterstown Avenue and was educated at Blackrock College. From his teenage days he well remembered the fantastic classical music concerts broadcast from Germany during the Second World War and also walking along the pier at Dún Laoghaire, to see the searchlights off Holyhead during that war. He became a noted conductor, working as assistant conductor with the then Radio Éireann Symphony Orchestra.

Between 1955 and 1970 he was the staff conductor for the RTÉ Concert Orchestra. Although short in stature, he was passionate in performance. He retired from RTÉ in 1991. Éimear's wife, Patricia Herbert, was a well-known concert pianist. In later years the couple lived in Sandyford; Éimear died in the Blackrock hospice in April 2013.

OWENS FAMILY

The Owens family have been noted dentists in Merrion for three generations. The practice was started by Dr Gerry Owens, who was born in 1914 and who qualified as a dentist in 1943 and went on to run his own practice, first in the Fitzwilliam Square area, then at Merrion Court, for a total of forty-six years. Dr Owens was also a renowned golfer; in 1939 he won the Irish Close Championship at Rosses Point in Co. Sligo and he went on to become a president of the Golfing Union of Ireland. He had a particular interest in promoting junior golf and he also had the rare honour of being a member of the Royal and Ancient Golf Club of St Andrews in Scotland. His first wife, Noël, died when she was just 37; Gerry died in August 1997, aged 83, and both of them are buried at Holmpatrick cemetery in his beloved Skerries in north Co. Dublin.

Dr Owens' son, Dr Gerald J. Owens, has served in the practice for many years and Gerald's son, Dr Roger Owens, is the third generation to maintain this remarkable dental continuity in Merrion.

JAMES EMERSON REYNOLDS

James Reynolds was born at 5 Booterstown Avenue in 1844 and qualified as a physician in Edinburgh in 1865. He practised for a short while, but soon turned his attention to chemistry. His forte was chemical analysis and he opened his first laboratory at the Royal Dublin Society. He made many pioneering discoveries as a chemist and he also had a thriving practice as an analyst. In 1870, he was made professor of chemistry at the Royal College of Surgeons in Ireland, then, in 1875, he was appointed to a similar position at Trinity College, Dublin. With his new job at Trinity, he had to give up his lucrative private practice as an analyst. He died in 1920.

ARMANDO TERRINONI

A well-known restaurateur, Armando lived at Booterstown Avenue in Booterstown. Brought up in Cori and Fuiggi, in central Italy, he had long been resident in Ireland, where he established Pizza Stop in Chatham Lane, just off Grafton Street in central Dublin, in 1982. It was long claimed to be the oldest established Italian pizzeria in Ireland, open daily for lunch, dinner and coffee. Armando died in St Vincent's University Hospital, Merrion, in September 2016, and in his will, published in early 2018, he left nearly €2 million. He was survived by his wife Grace and their three children, Isabella, Luca and Rocco.

JOE TREACY

Joe Treacy had a long connection with the old and now defunct First National Building Society (FNBS). He had joined it in 1954, when it was known as the Working Man's Benefit Building Society in Pearse Street, Dublin. He played a major role in the enormous expansion of the FNBS and he was one of the most prominent names in the now defunct building society movement in the 1970s and '80s. For many years he was managing director, before being appointed executive chairman. Joe Treacy then became the chair of the Rehab Group, a job that he held until 2006.

NINA TULLY

Nina Tully was long known as a dance teacher, even though her dance school, the Merrion School of Dancing, wasn't quite in Merrion. Her family home was on the Merrion Road, but in Ballsbridge rather than Merrion. Her dance school was in the back garden of the family home; she opened it in 1936 and kept it going until 1988, teaching several generations of girls from Merrion and the wider area the movements of classical dance. Nina died in 2000, aged 89.

SIMON WATSON

Noted international photographer Simon Watson comes from Booterstown. Now in his mid-40s, he has been resident in New York for the last twenty-five years, but also keeps a home in Dublin. Before he started on his worldwide travels, he studied film, painting and other visual arts before deciding to concentrate on photography. In 1998, he began a series of photographs showing the interior of properties in New Orleans after Hurricane Katrina. Then, eight years later, he began work on an even more harrowing series of photographs, taken in previously closed-off areas of Auschwitz concentration camp in Poland.

Over the past twenty years he has shown his work in many solo and group exhibitions in the US and Europe. His work has appeared in many international magazines and he also does a lot of work for top line advertising clients, mainly based in the US.

6

SCHOOLS AND YOUTH ORGANISATIONS

BLACKROCK COLLEGE

Blackrock College is a fee-paying Catholic secondary school for boys aged 13 to 18; the fees are considerable, around €7,000 a year for day students and about €18,000 a year for boarders.

The college dates back to 1860 when a French religious order, the Congregation of the Holy Ghost, set up the first of its five schools in Ireland. The founder was Fr Jules Leman, a French missionary priest. He had a dual purpose in running the new school, to train personnel for missionary work and to provide a first-class Catholic education for Irish boys. For many years the college was known locally as the French College.

For over forty years the college also provided training for entrants to the civil service and third-level education, where degrees were conferred by the old Royal University of Ireland. In time, as University College, Dublin, grew, it superseded university studies in Blackrock. The college was never a seminary, but some ordinations have taken place there.

For many years the college had a heavy clerical influence. In 1925, John Charles McQuaid joined the staff of the college and from then until 1931 he was Dean of Studies. From 1931 until 1939 he was president of the college, before being made Catholic Archbishop of Dublin. Today, the college is run by the Congregation of the Holy Ghost in conjunction with a dedicated group of lay people. The college now has over 1,000 students, with eighty-six teachers working in twenty-one departments. The most popular specialisations, in order, are biology, French, geography, business, history and accounting. About 94 per cent of all students go on to third-level studies.

Apart from the day students, the 100 or so boarders live in Williamstown Castle on the campus, which was built around 1780. The college places a heavy emphasis on sport, especially rugby, and the current Irish international team includes Ian Madigan, Luke Fitzgerald, Jordi Murphy and former captain Brian O'Driscoll, all of whom learned their rugby skills at Blackrock College. The college is also noted for the wide range of charitable activities undertaken by its students.

Blackrock College has had many distinguished teachers, including Éamon de Valera, who not only studied there but later became a maths teacher at the college. Michael Cusack, founder of the Gaelic Athletic Association, also taught there. The college has produced an astonishing array of talent among its former pupils, who've achieved fame in Ireland and internationally, as well as in many cases making their fortunes. Few if any other second-level schools have produced such a wealth of talent among their former pupils.

In literature, the college produced Brian O'Nolan, better known under his nom de plume Flann O'Brien;

Joseph O'Connor, contemporary writer; Liam O'Flaherty, best known for his work, *The Informer*, and Tim Pat Coogan, the last but one editor of the old *Irish Press*, now a distinguished historian. Also in the written word, Rory Carroll, David McWilliams, Paddy Murray and Paul Tansey were all former Rockmen.

In business, former pupils included Lochlann Quinn, a former chairman of AIB and co-founder of the Glen Dimplex group; Dr Brendan O'Regan, who transformed Shannon Airport, and Derek Quinlan, real estate investor.

When it comes to politics Blackrock College also has an outstanding record, including Éamon de Valera, a former student and then a teacher there; Vivion de Valera, one of his sons, who became managing director of the *Irish Press* group; Ruari Quinn, a former leader of the Labour Party; Rory O'Hanlon, a former Ceann Comhairle of the Dáil; James McNeill, second governor-general of the Irish Free State; and Michael Collins, an Irish ambassador. Another product of Willow Park and Blackrock College is David Andrews Jr, whose stage name is David McSavage, a well-known comedian, whose father was a former Foreign Affairs Minister.

In the legal profession, Blackrock College has produced many top-line lawyers, including several High Court judges, and Ronan Keane, a former chief justice of the Supreme Court. In more creative professions, past pupils have included Paul Costelloe and Pauric Sweeney, both fashion designers, and one of Ireland's best-known artists, Robert Ballagh. In the entertainment business, stars to have come out of Blackrock College include Des Bishop, comedian; Dave Fanning, broadcaster; Bob Geldof, who first found fame as the lead singer with the Boomtown Rats, then as organiser of the Live Aid concerts; Frank Kelly, actor; Ardal O'Hanlon, comic actor; and Ryan Tubridy, radio and television presenter at RTÉ.

Blackrock College has also produced innumerable sporting heroes, mainly but not exclusively in rugby, and these are listed separately in the sports chapter of this book.

The Blackrock College Union organises many reunions for past pupils who have graduated from the college up to fifty years ago. Many business, social and charitable events are staged each year in Ireland, the UK and the US. Much help is provided for missionary work by the Holy Ghost Order, while past pupils in need are also helped. If past pupils want to change direction in their careers, help is there for that, too. The Blackrock College Union is said to be the largest past pupils' union in either Ireland or Britain.

BOOTERSTOWN NATIONAL SCHOOL

This Church of Ireland school is in the grounds of the church of St Philip and St James in Cross Avenue and has four mainstream teachers, as well as support and resource teachers. The first schoolhouse was built close to the church in 1826, two years after the church had been consecrated. In the mid-1950s the old school was replaced by the present school building, which was opened by the then Taoiseach, Éamon de Valera, a long-time resident of Cross Avenue.

BOOTERSTOWN PARISH YOUTH CLUB

This youth club, in the old boys' national school in Grotto Place, just off the Rock Road in Booterstown, was started over forty years ago by Dessie Murphy and a number of other local people. The youth club is run on a voluntary basis and provides a wide range of activities for children from local schools and from the local area, aged from 4 upwards.

COLÁISTE EOIN

This Irish language Catholic voluntary secondary school for boys was established in Booterstown in 1969. It has about

450 students, taught by thirty-five teachers. The principal is Proinseas de Poire. Notable past teachers included Cliodna Cussen, sculptor and artist, and Tony Gregory, once an independent TD. Well-known past pupils include Liam Ó Maonlaí and Fiachna Ó Braonáin, both members of the Hothouse Flowers; Dan O'Brien, a noted economist, and author, historian and politician Aengus Ó Snodaigh.

The campus also includes Coláiste Íosagágain, an Irish language Catholic voluntary secondary school for girls.

GIRAFFE CRECHE

This creche has been on the Elm Park business campus since 2011 and caters for babies and children up to 5 years of age. It is part of a group that runs many creches in the Leinster region.

OUR LADY OF MERCY CONVENT SCHOOL

Located at Rosemount Terrace, off Booterstown Avenue, this Roman Catholic school, under the patronage of the Archdiocese of Dublin, provides classes for girls from junior infants up to sixth level. The principal at the time of writing is Siobhán Hanly.

ST ANDREW'S COLLEGE, BOOTERSTOWN

Founded in 1894 on St Stephen's Green as a Presbyterian boys' school, St Andrews is now a co-educational, inter-denominational international day school, located at Booterstown Avenue, Blackrock.

The school moved from St Stephen's Green to Wellington Place, Ballsbridge, in 1937 and stayed there until 1973, when it moved to its present location in Booterstown. The school now operates at both primary and secondary level and also offers the international Baccalaureate diploma course. It has fine sports facilities, including two hockey pitches, two rugby pitches, two tennis courts and an indoor sports hall and fitness centre. Past pupils have included Robert Briscoe, the first Jewish TD and a founding member of Fianna Fáil, as well as being a Lord Mayor of Dublin; Denis Johnston, the writer; Tom Dreaper, racehorse trainer; Ruth Gilligan and Eva Hewson, both actors; Senator David Norris and Cliff Taylor of *The Irish Times*, a former editor of the *Sunday Business Post*.

Currently, St Andrew's College has 997 students in its secondary school, with fees for day pupils similar to those in Blackrock College at around €6,500 a year. The college also has 255 pupils in its junior school.

ST ANNE'S INDUSTRIAL SCHOOL

This industrial school for Catholic girls was founded at Booterstown Avenue in 1870 by the Sisters of Mercy. Two years later, the school had a total of 114 inmates.

As well as school rooms and dormitories it also had a dairy. In the couple of years before 1875, two laundries were opened; the girls at the school had to work in the laundries, as well as in the garden, becoming proficient in everything from lacemaking to looking after pigs and poultry. Between 1895 and 1901 some of the girls were transferred from Booterstown to St Mary's industrial school in Blackrock, before some of them went back to Booterstown. The industrial school at Booterstown continued until the 1970s.

ST MARY'S BOYS' NATIONAL SCHOOL, BOOTERSTOWN

Founded in 1852, it has long provided excellence in primary education and now has over 300 pupils. The present school building dates back to 1968. Apart from the academic curriculum, the school provides many other activities, ranging from art to chess, even guitar lessons, while it also provides a wide range of sports, including athletics, Gaelic football, golf, hurling and tennis.

SHELTER REFERRAL BOTTLE BANK, MERRION

This bottle bank was established in 1973 by Martin McHale. For many years he was a senior executive in the old Irish Glass Bottle Company at Ringsend and he also became very involved in community activities through his interest in the Simon community. He started the bottle bank near the Merrion Gates in 1973 and one of its early managers was Dave Downes, now better known as an antiquarian bookseller in Stillorgan. When the bottle bank started, it employed men living below the poverty line to produce ground glass from discarded bottles to sell for industrial recycling.

SION HILL

Sion Hill, with its educational complex, gets its name from an old villa that once stood at the corner of Mount Merrion Avenue and Cross Avenue, which later became Sion Hill convent and school. The original owners of Sion Hill

named it after rare shrubs brought from the Holy Land. The original convent was built in the 1830s, while the present Sion Hill complex dates from the early 1990s. The larger building on the complex was St Catherine's College of Education for Home Economics, from 1929 until 2007. The run down of home economics teaching there began in 1990. The campus also had the Froebel College of Education from 1943 until 2013.

As for the Dominican College at Sion Hill, it has expanded much over the years. In its earliest years it catered for forty day pupils and eight boarders; it had eight nuns. By 1950 the number of day pupils had expanded to 120, with a further 130 boarders. The boarding school closed down in the 1960s and today the school caters for 350 day pupils, offering transition year studies, as well as junior and senior cycle studies. In the early twentieth century, girls at the Dominican College could study such subjects as bookkeeping, shorthand and scientific dressmaking, and even, in the late nineteenth century, courses in politeness.

Today's facilities are impressive, including an all-weather astro pitch and a multi-functional indoor sports hall, the St Thomas's library, an IT suite and a concert hall.

STRAND MONTESSORI SCHOOL

This Montessori School is located at Merrion Hall on the Strand Road, Merrion, where it has excellent indoor and outdoor facilities. At the time of writing, the staff comprised Nicky Doyle, Sarah Mannion and Niamh Rogers.

WILLOW PARK

Willow Park junior school is a Spiritan (Holy Ghost) that provides junior Catholic education to around 620 boys. It shares the Williamstown campus with Blackrock College and Willow Park first year; Willow Park is also a feeder school to Blackrock College, so many of the distinguished alumni of Blackrock College began their school days at Willow Park. The junior school building was opened in 2010, making it one of the most modern buildings on the entire campus.

7

SOCIAL AND MEDICAL

CARITAS CONVALESCENT CENTRE

The old Linden convalescent home in Stillorgan provided facilities for patients from many of the public hospitals in Dublin for over 120 years, but in 1993 it was announced that those facilities would be moved to the new purpose-built unit on the Merrion Road at Merrion, the Caritas Convalescent Centre. The facilities here include fifty-two beds, with all rooms en-suite, and 24-hour nursing care.

ST ANNE'S CONVENT, BOOTERSTOWN AVENUE

St Anne's Convent, opened in 1838, was Catherine Mcauley's seventh foundation. The first convent had been set up in Lower Baggot Street, Dublin, in 1827.

A committee of wealthy people from the Booterstown area, which had been set up to help the poor in the district, invited the nuns to take over the work. A typhus epidemic had overwhelmed the facilities provided by that group of wealthy people, so the Sisters of Mercy took over.

Land was donated for the building of the convent and a school by the Hon. Sidney Herbert, whose family owned much of the area. He also donated money for the construction of these buildings. In addition to the nuns in the convent and the children in the school, invalid Sisters from the convent in Lower Baggot Street came to Booterstown to convalesce. In addition, novices from that convent were brought out to Booterstown on the train for outings.

ST JOHN'S HOUSE OF REST, MERRION ROAD, MERRION

St John's was founded in 1869; members of the Trench family were closely connected with its foundation, including Jane, who was a trained nurse, and Richard Chevenix Trench, then Church of Ireland Archbishop of Dublin. It began in a very small house, offering temporary care, spiritual renewal and a change of diet to men, women and children in poor health. For its first fifty years, over a quarter of admissions were of male and female servants, about 4,000 in all, needing

rest and recuperation. Jane Trench was the lady in charge until 1919, when she died. After her death the Trench family influence declined.

In more recent times St John's has been a residential home providing care for retired and elderly women. A major extension to the premises is due to accommodate St Mary's, a similar home due to move there from Pembroke Park, as well as residents from the Molyneux Home. The chapel too in St John's is being refurbished. Once the new extension is completed, major refurbishments are due to be carried out the main part of the St John's building. Protestant Aid is also due to move to St John's from its present offices in Upper Leeson Street. The revamped and extended St John's is due to be ready before the end of 2018.

ST MARY'S CENTRE

St Mary's Centre on the Merrion Road at Merrion is a healthcare facility for elderly blind and visually impaired women and it includes two nursing homes, individual apartments and shared housing. The new buildings here were constructed in 1996.

The Sisters of Charity have been involved with the visually impaired since 1858, when they began in a small house in Dominic Street, Dublin. Within a year they had transferred to Portobello, where six Sisters cared for the blind residents. Then, in 1866, following prayers for a big house in a green field, what remained of Merrion Castle, together with all its land, was found. The site was acquired and a convent and a school for seventy blind children were built. Blind people took up residence at St Mary's for the first time on 14 August 1868.

Altogether, the new facilities were able to provide accommodation for around 250 people.

For the first time in Ireland, Braille was taught at St Mary's, in 1875. For many years subsequently the physical structures at St Mary's remained unaltered, but in 1960 a new school and a swimming pool were built. By the middle of the 1960s there were over 100 children at the school, mainly boarders. Major development work between 1994 and 1996 saw a whole range of new accommodation built.

St Mary's once had another claim to fame, dating back to its time in Portobello, when an orchestra was founded. After the move to Merrion, the orchestra gained in stature and the concerts given by the girls of St Mary's were very popular. St Mary's Orchestra produced many fine musicians, such as Nora Brady from Cork, noted in the late 1920s and early

1930s for being a harpist and pianist. In 1960, when Sister Vincent de Paul Read, who was in charge of the orchestra, became ill, the ensemble was dismantled.

ST VINCENT'S PRIVATE HOSPITAL

The private section of St Vincent's Hospital dates back to 1927, but it was established on the St Vincent's campus in 1974. It, St Vincent's University Hospital and St Michael's Hospital in Dún Laoghaire form the St Vincent's Healthcare Group, which was owned by the Religious Sisters of Charity until 2017.

The old private hospital on the St Vincent's campus closed down in 2010 and its facilities were transferred to the public

hospital and renamed the Nutley Wing. The brand new, state-of-the-art private hospital is nearby, just off the top of Herbert Avenue and built on the site of an old convent. It's a unique situation in Ireland for the public and private hospitals to be located on the same campus.

This new hospital has 236 inpatient beds, thirty-one day care beds and twenty-three day care oncology beds, and it's the largest privately run acute hospital in Dublin. The hospital has four main operating theatres, two minor ones, two endoscopy suites and an extensive range of diagnostic technologies, as well as twenty-four outpatient clinic rooms.

ST VINCENT'S UNIVERSITY HOSPITAL

St Vincent's University Hospital had its origins on St Stephen's Green, where the hospital was located from its foundation in 1834 until it moved to a brand new campus at Elm Park in Merrion in 1970. The land for the new hospital had been purchased in 1934 for £25,000 and permission to build the new hospital was given in 1948, so the gestation period was unusually lengthy.

In 1999, it was renamed a university hospital to reflect its position as a principal teaching hospital for UCD.

Today, the hospital is a regional centre for emergency medicine and medical care at inpatient and outpatient level. It's the national centre for liver transplants and adult cystic fibrosis. In 2017 the hospital carried out its 1,000th liver transplant. It's a training ground for medical staff, and students from UCD's medical degree courses also study here. The hospital has nearly 500 inpatient suites. A major extension building was completed in 2006, including a new emergency department. The next major construction project will be the new National Maternity Hospital, due to move to St Vincent's from its present site in Holles Street.

A number of research groups are linked to clinical departments within the hospital, which has also seen a number of ground-breaking surgical procedures, and there are close academic links with UCD.

8

CHURCHES

CHURCH OF THE ASSUMPTION, BOOTERSTOWN AVENUE

The origins of this church go back to 1686, when the first chapel was founded here, and to 1755, when Fr Archbold started the first parish register in Booterstown. He died four years later and was succeeded by the Revd Mathias Kelly, a very learned and zealous priest, who came to live in the area. His address was given as Old Merrion. After he died in 1775, he was succeeded by Fr James Nicholson and it was in 1787, during Fr Nicholson's incumbency, that the parish of Booterstown, Donnybrook and Dundrum was divided. Donnybrook became a separate parish to Booterstown, while Booterstown, still largely rural, continued to include Blackrock, Stillorgan and Dundrum.

Father Nicholson had a small chapel in Booterstown, beside which he built a parochial house. Booterstown was still considered too insignificant to become a parish in its own right. He died in 1794 and eventually, in 1811, Fr Michael Ryan was appointed the parish priest of Booterstown. He made great progress with the new church, in Booterstown Avenue. Its foundation stone was laid on 6 August 1812 and

the church was built largely thanks to the interventions of Mrs Barbara Verschoyle, commemorated by an elaborate plaque inside the church. It was funded by Richard, the 7th Viscount Fitzwilliam of Merrion. The new church was dedicated on 15 August 1813, great care having been taken with its external appearance so as not to annoy Protestants in the area. It was known as St Mary's from 1813 until 1950, when it became known as the Church of the Assumption. Just three years after the church was dedicated, the 7th Viscount died, bringing to an end the Fitzwilliam line, which had been influential in the area for the previous 500 years. They had been one of the most prominent Catholic families in Ireland.

Behind the church, which doesn't face the road but which has been improved and enlarged over the years, is the presbytery.

MERRION CHAPEL OF EASE

In the early part of the twentieth century, Mrs Anne M. Doyle, who owned a grocery and wine shop in Merrion, donated the site to the Archbishop of Dublin, for the eventual construction of a new church. Merrion was then within the parish of Booterstown. Then in 1923, Matthew McCabe, who lived in Trimleston, bought the freehold interest in the site from the Pembroke estate for the Archbishop of Dublin. Fundraising began for the proposed new church in the early 1920s, but it took thirty years for it to materialise.

The first major fundraising came in September 1925, when the Merrion Bazaar and Carnival was held in the grounds of the convent of the Sisters of Mercy at Booterstown. The advent of the Second World War in 1939 meant a further delay in building a proper church and during the Emergency and indeed right up to 1951 parishioners in Merrion had the use of allotments on the church site.

In 1940, as soon as Revd John Charles McQuaid, who had been president of Blackrock College, was made the Catholic Archbishop of Dublin, he authorised the building of a temporary wooden church at Merrion. The walls were wooden, but the roof was tin, so inevitably, it became known as the 'Tin Church'. It opened on 18 November 1940; it had a wooden tabernacle and could seat 600 parishioners. A decade later, Archbishop McQuaid authorised the construction of a permanent church.

The project manager was Fr Dan Daly from Booterstown. Parishioners who had raised funds for the new church felt they were entitled to a say in its design, but Archbishop McQuaid had his own views, and he made sure that these prevailed. The Hiberno–Romanesque style popular in Ireland during the 1950s was the one used, but it has often been criticised as being a mish-mash of many different architectural styles. The archbishop also insisted on a replica round tower, complete with bell, being built beside the church and this too was the subject of controversy. The church was blessed and opened by Archbishop McQuaid on 13 December 1953. Officially, it was a chapel of ease, because Merrion didn't become a parish in its own right until 1964.

When the church opened in 1953, the first priest was Fr Daniel Daly, assisted by Fr Patrick Dargan. In 2008 the parish became the first in Ireland to be run by Opus Dei. The decision to hand over the parish had been taken by the Archbishop of Dublin, Diarmuid Martin, without any consultation with the priests or the people of the parish. The current parish priest is the Very Revd Fergus O'Connor, while the curate is Revd James Hurley.

The church was renovated in 2012, with the grounds being renovated two years later, and it is the centre of what is now known as the Merrion Road parish. In 2016, parking in the church grounds was handed over to a privately owned parking company, a move instigated by what happened during a funeral. So many commuters had parked their cars there that mourners at the funeral couldn't park their cars. People now have to pay to park their cars in the church grounds, although there is a period of grace – 45 minutes' free parking.

In recent years, one of the highest profile funerals at Our Lady Queen of Peace was that of 25-year-old Daniel Marshall, in July 2014. He was the son of well-known hairstylist David Marshall and Jackie Rafter, a former model turned socialite. Daniel had been heavily into drugs and he had been found dead in the toilets of the Fitzwilliam Hotel on St Stephen's Green. Celebrities who attended the funeral included snooker player Ken Doherty, RTÉ radio presenter Dave Fanning, former owner of Black Tie Niall O'Farrell, and singer Dickie Rock.

ST PHILIP AND ST JAMES, CROSS AVENUE

The construction of this Church of Ireland church came in the wake of the setting up of Booterstown parish in May 1821. The area had been part of the extensive parish of St Mary's in Anglesea Road in Donnybrook and the decision was made to create the new parish of Booterstown because so many large, detached houses were being built there.

The two men responsible for creating the new parish were the 11th Earl of Pembroke, who owned the land, and a well-known banker called James Digges La Touche. The Earl of Pembroke also provided £1,000 for building a new church, which was designed in a very distinctive style by Joseph Welland, then the supervising architect in the Church of Ireland, and John Bowden. The church building has many standout Gothic Revival architectural features, as it is full of parapets and pinnacles, at that time much in favour for new Church of Ireland churches. The cost of building the new church came to £4,615 7s 8d and 1 farthing. The church was consecrated on 16 May 1824.

In 1867, the church was enlarged with the addition of a chancel and a south transept, while in 1876 further extensions were made, including a north transept and an organ chamber. The substantial organ was restored in the mid-twentieth century. Those extensions created the church that's known today, which can seat 500 people, although one striking addition was made in the 1960s, the mosaic of Christ Blessing the Children, a memorial commissioned by Henry Dowse as a tribute to his wife.

Close by the church is Booterstown national school, the parish centre, the rectory and the Barrett Cheshire Home.

9

HOTELS, PUBS AND RESTAURANTS

BOOTERSTOWN'S FAKE HOTEL

In 2016 and 2017, Booterstown got an entirely new hotel – the Hotel View Villa – which only existed as a website in order to scam people from India and elsewhere in Asia into paying money to secure work permits in Ireland. On its website, the hotel described itself as being modern and just a short distance from St Stephen's Green and Grafton Street. But it inadvertently gave the game away when it said that its location on Booterstown Avenue overlooked the Grand Canal!

The actual address of the hotel was a house in Booterstown Avenue, whose occupants knew nothing of the alleged hotel, whose website had been set up to trick people into thinking it was a legitimate business. The website even had a raft of fake testimonies from guests who had 'stayed' at the Hotel View Villa. Local gardaí said they had heard nothing about the fake hotel.

GLEESON'S HOTEL

The well-known Gleeson's pub on Booterstown Avenue is planning to go into the hotel business. In July 2017, it announced that it plans to spend €1.6 million developing a boutique hotel with sixteen bedrooms beside the existing pub. Subject to planning approval, it was estimated likely to be 2019 before the new hotel opened.

ST HELEN'S HOTEL

The ultra-luxurious hotel, in the Blu Radisson group, may be just off the main Stillorgan Road but it is actually in Booterstown. The fine house in which the hotel is located dates back to 1750, when it was constructed as Seamount. Later, the house was renamed St Helen's and, for many years during the nineteenth century, was home to the Right Hon. Hugh Gough; a Limerick man who had a distinguished career in the British Army. From the mid-1920s until 1988, the property was owned by the Christian Brothers, but in 1988 the site was sold to a property developer. A preservation order was placed on the house, which became the St Helen's Hotel, with a fine range of public rooms and bedrooms. For the last twenty years it has had a reputation as one of the most luxurious hotels in Dublin.

Its facilities include 126 deluxe bedrooms and twenty-five business class suites, the Talavera restaurant with its Italian cuisine, the Le Panto private dining suite and the Orangerie bar and lounge, which have full menus.

TARA TOWERS HOTEL

This multi-storey hotel has long been a fixture on the Merrion Road, as it was built in 1970. It stands on a site of around 0.6 ha and has its own parking. The hotel was built by the Doyle Hotel Group and for many years has been a popular venue for people seeking budget hotel accommodation, as well as bar and dining facilities.

The hotel was bought in 2016 for €13.2 million by the Dalata Hotel Group, which in July 2017 submitted a planning application to demolish the existing hotel and replace it with a 140-bedroom four-star Maldron Hotel. The scheme will also include seventy residential units and a basement car park. The present Tara Towers Hotel was expected to close towards the end of 2018 and, if the

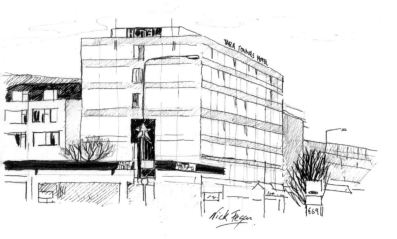

planning application was successful, it would take up to two years to develop the replacement hotel.

COACH AND HORSES INN

This pub was on the Merrion Road, directly opposite what is now the Merrion Gates. It opened in the mid-nineteenth century to cater for the growing amount of traffic on the Merrion Road, as well as traffic to the then Merrion railway station. Some years after the Sisters of Charity had opened their blind asylum and industrial school on the Merrion Road, they bought the pub and incorporated it into their existing premises. In 1995, the old pub was demolished to make way for new accommodation on the St Mary's site, for elderly and blind people.

GLEESON'S

Gleeson's pub in Booterstown Avenue has long been a watering place for many southsiders, including former students of Blackrock College who developed an affinity for the pub when they were pupils at the college, and executives of many organisations, such as RTÉ.

The pub has a long history, going back well over a century. It was originally called Murphy's and was as well-known for having a grocery shop as it was for being a pub. Frank Gleeson, who sold a pub in Parnell Street, Dublin, in 1920 to buy a farm in Newcastle, Co. Dublin, and then went on to own a shop in Celbridge for many years, bought Murphy's pub in Booterstown in 1954. He paid £6,250 for the premises and the first thing he did after taking possession on 2 December 1954 was to close down the grocery shop.

The first customer to come in was a woman looking for a loaf of bread and some paraffin. When she was told that those items were no longer on sale, she retorted, 'Where do you think you are, Grafton Street?' Murphy's had been an old style country pub, which included a counter where such items as bread, butter, sugar, tea and paraffin oil had been sold.

In 1955, Frank Gleeson borrowed £4,500 to add a lounge bar to the pub. He also bought an adjoining couple of houses, where the pub car park is now situated. Frank and his wife Nora reared their three sons and five daughters in the fourteen rooms over the pub and today the pub has been

passed on to two of Frank Gleeson's grandchildren, Ciaran and John, having been run for many years by Frank Gleeson's son, also Frank. In recent times the current Frank Gleeson has been chairman of the Licensed Vintners' Association in Dublin.

In 1963, Nora decided that the pub should start serving hot food at lunchtime and these hot meals, with refreshments, became popular with local business people, particularly those working in the advertising industry. In recent years Gleeson's has also had a night-time restaurant, while becoming noted for its food corner selling a wide range of ready-prepared take-home meals.

The original Frank Gleeson died in 2012, after being married to Nora for fifty-seven years. In August 2017, Nora celebrated her 90th birthday.

One of Ireland's best-known public figures, Dr T.K. Whitaker, who drafted the economic plan that got Ireland out of recession in the late 1950s and early 1960s and turned the country into a modern economy, had his 100th birthday lunch in Gleeson's on 8 December 2016. Among the many people who popped in to congratulate him was the then Taoiseach, Enda Kenny. Less than a month after that lunch, Ken Whitaker died.

MERRION INN

The Merrion Inn, on the Merrion Road opposite St Vincent's Hospital, is a long-established pub that has been owned by the McCormack family since 1991. Before it was taken over by the McCormack family it was known as T.V. Brady's. But the pub that's on the site today is brand new, the result of a disastrous fire in June 2014. The fire started in a back kitchen area and spread rapidly, doing extensive damage to the first floor and the roof, while the ground floor suffered much water damage.

Father and son, Eamonn and Fearghus McCormack, and their staff worked diligently to ensure the pub came back into operation. Within twelve months it was back in action, giving the Merrion area a brand new pub.

OLD PUNCH BOWL

This is the oldest pub in the district, dating back to 1779 when it was opened by William Scully, who traded under his own name. In the late eighteenth century and well into the nineteenth century, funeral processions going from Dublin to Dean's Grange cemetery stopped at this halfway stage for refreshments. The stop was brief, about 10 minutes, just enough time for the mourners to get a quick drink and for the horses to be fed and watered. The then owner devised a hot drink, similar to mulled wine, and served it from a silver goblet on the counter. So, in 1879, when the pub was celebrating its first century, the name was changed to the Old Punch Bowl.

For many years, the pub competed with one on the opposite side of Booterstown Avenue, where it meets the Rock Road, called McCabe's. The man who owned that pub was a local councillor of that name and he was also responsible for the development of the nearby McCabe's Villas.

In its early days, what is now the Old Punch Bowl served another purpose. Underground tunnels ran from close to the pub to the foreshore and these were used for extensive smuggling. In those days, the police barracks was next door to the pub and all this smuggling went on without the police having any idea of the illicit trade taking place right on their doorstep.

In more recent times, the Old Punch Bowl has had many owners, a total of eight between 1960 and the present day. The present owner, Joe O'Rorke, bought the pub in May 1996 from Ken Fetherston. The pub is still very traditional in appearance, with many old photographs and front pages from the late 1930s from the long defunct *Irish Press* newspaper. It even has a library and patrons are encouraged to take a book, while it also has a games room and a heated beer garden. The pub is also noted for its food, served in the ground-floor bar, a traditional bar

for rugby supporters, and an upstairs function suite, the Seaview Suite, which can accommodate up to 170 people standing. This room is also used for musical events and has attracted many famed musicians, including Christy Moore and Luka Bloom.

WILLIAMSTOWN

The Rock Road in Williamstown, the main road to Blackrock, was long renowned for its pub, although this hasn't existed for the past twenty years.

Until 1903, Willimstown was on the Blackrock College side of Rock Road. But when Blackrock College started demolishing the main road properties, including Castledawson Avenue, in 1903, to enhance the college frontage, the two pubs beside the college were demolished. When the village was moved to the seaward side of Rock Road, only one survived the change, to reinvent itself in its new location, but with the same name, Keegan's.

The pub subsequently went under a number of names, including Kennedy's, from 1946 until 1955. It then went under a variety of other names, including Deasy's, Martin's and Grainger's, before becoming a well-known watering hole under the name of Brady's. From 1996 for nearly a decade it was known as Bergkamp's. That was its last incarnation as a pub; these days, the building is occupied by a firm of architects, Frank Ennis & Associates, but the front of the building still shows many signs of the old pub façade.

BATZ

The Batz outlet in Booterstown Avenue specialised in à la carte catering but has long been closed. At the time of writing, the two retail outlets on either side are also derelict.

BIANCONI'S

This family run Italian-style restaurant has been open on the Merrion Road, close to the church, for nearly fifteen years. It offers all-day menus.

KALDI'S

This is another recent addition to Booterstown Avenue and has quickly built up a reputation as a coffee hotspot serving first-class coffee since it opened in early 2017. Food specialities include a popular porridge dish.

MERRION SHOPPING CENTRE

The centre has an all-day bistro called Encore, formerly Garfields, which is very popular with people taking time out from doing their shopping in the centre. It also offers a wide range of salads and sandwiches to take out.

SWEET

This charming establishment at 45 Booterstown Avenue, close to St Andrew's College, has been open since September 2015 and has an excellent reputation for its sweet dishes and also for its bread. Its signature dishes include squidgy browns, chocolate cakes and what have been described as the 'most amazing' bakery products. It also serves Fixx coffee and Teddy's ice cream and milkshakes.

WONG'S KITCHEN

This takeaway based on the Rock Road at Williamstown is popular for its dishes based on modern and classic Chinese cuisine.

10

SHOPS AND BUSINESSES

BOOTERSTOWN HOUSE

Once the headquarters of the old and now defunct First National Building Society, this office block just off the foot of Booterstown Avenue houses a number of business concerns. These include Orix Aviation, whose services cover all aspects of aircraft operation, including sales, financial and administration. It has an impressive list of global clients, airlines that are known the world over, including Ryanair, British Airways, easyJet, Lufthansa, SAS, TUI, Emirates, Etihad, Air China and Qantas.

Another important company at Booterstown House is IFG, a financial services company, which occupies one of the two blocks that made up the former First National headquarters, its name Skehan House replaced by Booterstown House in 2001. In addition to the main office buildings, a small development of one- and two-bedroom apartments was constructed at nearby Booterstown Hall in 2009.

BROWN'S NEWSAGENTS, MERRION ROAD

Brown's Newsagents on the Merrion Road, just past Our Lady's Queen of Peace church, dates back to 1908 and is the oldest retail business in Merrion and Booterstown.

It was started by William and Martha Brown and continued by their children, Arthur and Rosanna. Arthur was also noted for his ancient Morris Minor car. These days, the shop is run by Rose Brown, granddaughter of the founders, and her husband, Tony McDonald; Rose and Tony have four children, two boys and two girls. The present-day shop, besides selling newspapers and magazines, has a wide range of other goods, including sweets and religious material.

This small row of shops once had a sub post office for Merrion, but this closed down in May 1980 and its premises were taken over by the medical centre. The post office had long been a feature of the Merrion Road here, as it had opened just before the start of the First World War, not long after Brown's shop had been started.

CARROLL & KINSELLA

This well-known car firm, which has held one of Ireland's longest-serving Toyota dealerships (over forty years), has an impressive showroom on the Rock Road at Williamstown, although the firm describes itself as being in Blackrock. In its showrooms an extensive range of Toyota cars and commercial vehicles are on show. Joe Kinsella is the managing director, while Ken Carey is sales director and Joe Kinsella junior is the sales manager. Apart from its new vehicles, Carroll & Kinsella is also noted for its selection of pre-used vehicles. In addition to its showrooms on the Rock Road, it also has a base at the Deansgrange business park, where its service department is located.

CIRCUSES

The Circus Field in Booterstown, close to the Martello tower, was for a long time used by two of Ireland's leading circus companies, Duffy's and Fossetts. The former usually pitched camp on the field in June or July each year, while Fossetts arrived in October. In recent years, the tents have become much bigger; close on twenty years ago, Charles O'Brien of Fossetts said that their big tent held 750 people, whereas in the old days it was much smaller, holding 300. He also said that television had had a big effect on circus performances, which used to happen at a slower pace. Television had the effect of making the performances quicker and more immediate. However, a big change came to circus' in Ireland at the start of 2018, when performances by animals were banned.

CLARKE'S CONVENIENCE STORE

This shop at 87 Booterstown Avenue, close to St Andrew's College, is a long-established shop, small but busy, which combines a newsagents, deli and convenience outlet.

ESRAS FILMS

This well-known TV production company is based on the Booterstown side of Mount Merrion Avenue; its CEO is Peter Kelly. The name Esras is derived from the word for Druid in Celtic mythology. Since 1996, Esras Films has made many award-winning productions for RTÉ and TG4 in the Republic and for many broadcasters outside the Republic, from the BBC in Northern Ireland to CNN and Al Jazeera. The company has extensive inhouse production facilities, editing and post-production suites, and besides its work in television it also provides extensive audio-visual facilities.

FERRIS WHEELS

The Ferris Wheels bicycle shop has been trading on the Rock Road at Booterstown, close to Booterstown Avenue, for over thirty years. Now in the third generation of the Ferris family, the shop has long been selling bikes to customers, from Dublin and beyond, and giving advice on a wide range of cycling issues. A full range of accessories is also available, while Ferris Wheels also provides a full repair service, from puncture repair to a complete bike rebuild. It is not to be confused with a bike shop of the same name in Jamaica Plain, Minnesota! This same stretch of the Rock Road is also occupied by retail outlets, DNG estate agents, Firehouse pizzas, the Your Shop outlet and Jordan's Barbers.

GERMAN EMBASSY

The German Embassy is at Trimleston Avenue in Booterstown. Work began on planning and designing the new embassy in 1977, so that it could replace the previous embassy in Northumberland Road, Ballsbridge. The new embassy in Booterstown took three years to build and was officially opened on 15 November 1984. As the building is now nearing forty years old, it is, at the time of writing, undergoing a major refurbishment. There will be a couple of changes outside, but the general exterior of the building and the site will remain unchanged, as most of the refurbishment is being done to the interior.

The current German ambassador to Ireland is Mrs Deike Potzel, who took up the position at the end of 2017, succeeding Matthias Höpfner. Links are close between Ireland and Germany. Ireland has 300 German companies, employing a total of 20,000 people and half a million German tourists visit Ireland annually. The Germany Embassy in Booterstown and the Japanese Embassy in Merrion are the only two diplomatic locations in the area.

GOWAN GROUP

This well-known group, which is involved in a wide range of activities including kitchen appliances and Senator windows, has its headquarters in Herbert Avenue, Merrion. The group was founded in 1969 by Con Smith, who was killed in the Staines air crash near Heathrow Airport, London, in 1972. His widow, Gemma, went on to marry another well-known businessman, Michael Maughan, who made his name in the advertising business. Between them, they own 46 per cent of the Gowan Group, while Gemma's four daughters from her first marriage are also shareholders. Also on Herbert Avenue, with frontage on the main Merrion Road, is Gowan Motors, which specialises in selling new cars from the Honda, KIA, Opel and Peugeot marques, as well as doing Citroën aftersales. Gowan Motors has been a well-established name in motoring circles for over forty years.

Part of what is now the Gowan Motors premises was once Treacy's general grocery shop, one of the old-style shops in Merrion and Booterstown that have long since disappeared. Gowan Motors also absorbed the dairy once run by the Lewis family and their big walled garden, which is now used for car parking.

JAPANESE EMBASSY

Ireland has had diplomatic relations with Japan since 1957; from 1970 until 1992, the Japanese Embassy in Dublin was in Ailesbury Road, but in that latter year it moved to the Nutley Building, beside the Merrion Shopping Centre. The Japanese ambassador is Mori Mujoshi. She and her staff oversee a wide range of activities, including support for Irish companies that want to invest in Japan, and Irish tourists who want to visit the country. In December 2017, about 100 Irish people sat the Japanese language proficiency test, which has been organised in Dublin for nearly a decade now. Apart from business relations between the two countries, the embassy is also involved in a wide range of cultural exchanges between Ireland and Japan.

LONGFORD HOUSE

Longford House on the Merrion Road, close to Brown's Newsagents, was a long-established general haberdashery and post office. In 1884, Margaret Ryan bought the shop for £500. At that same time a number of Victorian red brick houses, nos 242 to 248, were built, complementing a number of two-room cottages that had been built in this immediate area in 1855. Margaret called her new shop Longford House after Longford Terrace in Monkstown, Co. Dublin, where she had been companion to a wealthy woman. When that woman died, she left Margaret a substantial amount of money, enabling her to buy the shop on the Merrion Road.

Today, the old shop houses the premises of the Merrion Gates Medical Centre, which opened in 1995 and provides a wide range of GP Services. Another company involved in health, Hidden Hearing, is located between the medical centre and Brown's. The Hidden Hearing branch here was opened in the summer of 2013 by singer Daniel O'Donnell. Other old businesses in Merrion that are also long gone include the old Merrion Dairy and Joan's shop, which was demolished in the 1960s.

McCABE'S

McCabe's wine shop at the corner of Mount Merrion Avenue and Cross Avenue was long a favourite spot for wine lovers, who could find a truly excellent selection of vintages from all over the world. But sadly for the area's wine aficionados, the shop is now closed and the business transferred to the Gables restaurant and wine bar in Foxrock village.

Brothers Jim and John McCabe had moved from the North to become students at Blackrock College. They acquired the block on the corner of Cross Avenue, just opposite Sion Hill. As both of the brothers had been to Blackrock College, they decided to call the newsagents shop Straneys. They ran the shop for a couple of years with the help of two young ladies called Helen and Frances, but leased it out in 1988–89. But all the owners since, including Joe, Ciarán, Tom and Roddy, have kept the same name, Straneys, over the door.

The McCabe brothers also tried a sandwich bar called Mr Sub, not unlike Subway today. But it was ahead of its time and lost money, so the outlet became the first shop for Butler's Pantry, which Eileen Bergin opened about 1987. It was the first shop of many in the group.

The pièce de résistance, the wine shop, opened in 1986 and for many years it was a great shop, well-stocked, that drew wine enthusiasts from far and near. John and Jim remember that on the day they opened, the first five people to come to the shop said it was in a bad location, because it was neither in Blackrock nor Stillorgan, while the following five said that it was in a great location, because it was in neither place!

The introduction of a bus lane by the county council had a damaging effect on the business as customers could no longer park outside. The brothers also failed on numerous occasions to get planning permission to revamp the building, so closure was inevitable. The old wine shop is still empty, but the McCabe brothers still own the building and Straney's and the Butler's Pantry outlets are still going strong.

At the time of going to press, the McCabes were in the process of selling the building.

MERRION BRICKWORKS

For much of the eighteenth century Merrion was the centre of much brick-making activity, as the great squares and streets of Georgian Dublin were developed. The Merrion Brickworks were substantial and preceded similar brick-making activity at nearby Sandymount, which was originally called Bricktown. Today, there is no trace left of either brickworks, which had once been so prominent in this part of south Co. Dublin.

In the early eighteenth century Dublin had several brickworks, but the most extensive were Lord Merrion's brickfields, on an extensive strip of land that stretched from Merrion Castle to what became Brickfield Town, later Sandymount. These brickfields were marked on a map as early as 1706. A survey in 1762 of the Pembroke estate showed a list of owners and tenants on the brickfields. When Merrion Square and surrounding streets were being built in the later eighteenth century, all the russet-coloured bricks used on the façades of the houses, tens of thousands of bricks, came from the Merrion brickfields. But the urban brickfields in Dublin and Cork were considered such a health hazard that an Act of Parliament was passed in 1771 banishing brickworks from those two cities. By 1794 a map of the Pembroke estate showed the abandoned brick holes, from which the clay had been extracted, filled with water. Those brick holes were roughly on a line with present-day Sandymount Avenue.

MERRION HALL

Merrion Hall on Strand Road in Merrion – not Sandymount! – was opened in 1973. The building was constructed on a site that was prone to flooding, but the many concerns expressed at the time about the flood risk turned out to be unduly alarmist, even though the building is well below the level of Strand Road.

It replaced the riding stables that had existed in the grounds of the old Merrion Hall for many years. In the 1960s these riding stables were run by the Flavin family; the father was an Englishman who worked for Hammond Lane and his daughter was keen on horse riding. Before the Flavins, the riding stables had been run by a man called Eddie Gallagher.

When Merrion Hall opened, it housed the headquarters of Irish Shipping, the State-owned shipping line that closed down in 1984 following huge losses. Merrion Hall was also the base for many years for Coras Tráchtála, the old board for exporting, which closed down in 1998. It was subsequently occupied by Enterprise Ireland until it moved to its present headquarters in East Point Business Park. Today, Merrion Hall is occupied by a number of commercial companies, including the Outsource Services group.

MERRION HOUSE

This office block, built in the 1970s, is almost opposite the Tara Towers Hotel, a brutalist concrete assembly devoid of any design merit whatsoever that replaced the Art Deco Imco building. Today, Merrion House contains a number of firms, including Jacobs Engineering, an Irish-based but international engineering design company founded in 1974, which has its headquarters in Merrion House.

MERRION ROAD OFFICE BLOCK

A long vacant office block on the Merrion Road in Merrion was rented in 2015 to Willis, a global insurance broker, and to Wipro, an Indian IT consultancy firm. Another big company to set up nearby in the Elm Park development is Allianz, the insurance company, which established its Dublin HQ there, employing over 500 people. In 2013, Novartis, the world's second largest pharmaceutical company, set up its Dublin regional business services centre in Elm Park.

MERRION SHOPPING CENTRE

The Merrion Shopping Centre was built on derelict land at the corner of the Merrion Road and Nutley Lane in 1985–86; it opened in 1987 and remains the only shopping centre in the district. The centrepiece has always been the supermarket, which started off as Quinnsworth but, following a takeover in 1997, was renamed Tesco. It still trades as Tesco today and remains a Mecca for shoppers. Extensive free parking is one of the 'draws'. The supermarket has been expanded over the years by taking over various other retailers, including the Wordsworth bookshop. Today, in addition to the Tesco supermarket, the Merrion Shopping Centre has about twenty other retailers, including a restaurant.

Alongside the shopping centre substantial office accommodation was built; the various occupiers include the Japanese Embassy.

NUTLEY NEWSAGENTS

This shop has been in the Merrion Shopping Centre since the centre opened and it remains probably the best-known retail outlet in the centre, after Tesco. The directors of Nutley Newsgagents are Gareth Kearns and Paul Murphy. The shop has an enviable range of stock, offering everything from newspapers, magazines and books to stationery and greeting cards. Many customers over the years have often compared it to a country newsagents, such is the selection.

Another well-known retailer in the centre, although now retired, was Willie O'Connor, who ran the jewellery shop for many years. Under its new owners, it traded as Remané jewellers, which was started in Dún Laoghaire over seventy years ago and which traded in the Dún Laoghaire Shopping Centre for thirty-eight years. Remané has since closed down in the centre, replaced by Paddy Electronics

Other well-known retailers in the Merrion Shopping Centre include Peter Mark ladies' hairdressers, Tony Walsh pharmacy, Dwyer's family butchers and Merrion Hardware, which for a small shop has an amazing stock of household items. Walsh's pharmacy and the Nutley Newsagents are two of the longest established retail outlets in the centre.

HOMAN O'BRIEN

This leading engineering practice has been trading for over sixty years and specialises in the design and management of mechanical, electrical and lift services for all types of buildings. It is currently based at 89 Booterstown Avenue, constructed in 1970, just off Booterstown Avenue.

OLD SHOPS IN BOOTERSTOWN AVENUE

Among the old shops long gone in Booterstown Avenue was Fitzells at No. 87, a high-class family grocer and provision merchant run by the Fitzell family. Another old-time shop was the Woodville Dairy, run by a man called Woods. He was called 'Rubber Neck' by local people, as he had a long neck that he could swivel. He also owned a parrot and on one occasion, when it went missing, he put up a notice in his shop window which read: 'Parrot Missing, last seen on the telegraph wire, reciting "Buy your goods at Woods"'. A second dairy in Booterstown Avenue, at nos 79 and 89, was

the Primrose Dairy run by Francis Graham. He delivered 'pure new milk, twice daily' from his own herd of cows. Yet another of the old-style shops was Garvey's hardware store, which displayed many of its lines, such as watering cans and brushes, on the façade of the shop and on the pavement.

OLD SHOPS ON ROCK ROAD

Old shops on the Rock Road corner of Booterstown Avenue included Doyle's butchers shop, where the Ferris Wheels cycle shop is now based. Next door to the butchers was McMahon's the chemists, while upstairs Tommy Basquille ran a bakery business, producing excellent cakes and brown bread. On the corner was Cassidy's high-class grocery shop, long since demolished. A mini market now stands on the site.

O'NEILL'S BUILDING FIRM

This firm, which once specialised in building, carpentry, conservatories and extensions, was based on the Rock Road at Williamstown. Modern-day firms along this section of the Rock Road include Frank Ennis & Associates, architects, based in what was the old pub at Williamstown. Two other architectural practices are also based on the Rock Road, Niall Montgomery & Partners and Brady & Associates, while JSA Architects is nearby, at Booterstown Avenue. The Rock Road has also been long known for having Ireland's largest Irish-owned damp proofing company, The Damp Store. The Rock Road also had a sub post office, which opened just before the start of the First World War in 1914 and which traded for many years, until 1980, when it closed, according to An Post's museum and archive section.

PETIT FASHION SHOP

The row of shops on the Merrion Road, almost beside the Catholic church, is like a 'Little Italy' in the middle of Merrion. Besides the Italian-style Bianconi restaurant, the Petit shop is also Italian-inspired in its clothes for babies, children and teenagers. Families can have matching outfits, with accessories to match, and Petit brings that tremendous sense of Italian style to its clothes. According to Paola Macari, the Petit shop has been trading for some thirteen years. Next door to this shop, and the first shop in this row, nearest the church, is a branch of the Bank of Ireland. The row of shops here once had a sub post office.

WORDSWORTH

When it comes to the book trade in Merrion, books gave way to booze. The Wordsworth bookshop was very successful in the Merrion Shopping Centre for the best part of fifteen years, but over ten years ago it and a number of retailers on the Merrion Road side of the shopping centre had to close because their space was required for an expansion of Tesco. Wordsworth had been a successful bookseller but had to pull down the shutters. What is now the off-licence section of Tesco was once the Wordsworth bookshop. The closure of Wordsworth meant that Merrion and Booterstown had lost their only bookshop, although the Nutley Newsagents in the shopping centre still stocks some books.

11

NATURE AND WILDLIFE

BIRDWATCHING

Booterstown Marsh is an ideal site for bird watching, with mallard, moorhens and teals regularly seen in the marsh, while waders often make their way from Sandymount Strand, hopping across the railway line to reach the marsh. Other bird species that breed either in the marsh or close by include blackbirds, buntings, dunnocks and wrens. Birdlife can be seen anywhere on the marsh as well as on the two man-made islands. Some notable moments in birdwatching have taken place on Booterstown marsh, including the sighting of a great spotted woodpecker, a rare but magnificent bird, which was spotted on 16 October 1949. The marsh has been managed by An Taisce since 1970.

BOOTERSTOWN MARSH

Booterstown Marsh is 4.3 hectares of salt marsh and muds, the only salt marsh and the only bird sanctuary in south Dublin Bay. It's just north of Booterstown DART station and its car park and lies between the railway line and the main Rock Road.

It's fed with fresh water from the Nutley Stream as well as occasionally from the Trimleston Stream, while a limited amount of seawater flows in beneath the railway embankment. The marsh has two low-lying mud islands, which were created in 2006 and provide resting and roosting areas for birds.

Originally, the area occupied by the marsh was open to Merrion Strand and was part of a marsh area that stretched all the way from Sandymount to Blackrock. Much of this original marsh has been lost over the years due to reclamation work. The current Booterstown Marsh was formed when the Westland Row to Dun Leary railway line was built in 1834. The line was built on an embankment, protected by a granite seawall. This resulted in a tidal lagoon covering nearly 30 hectares, but over the following decades much of this lagoon was filled in, leaving only Booterstown Marsh subject to flooding by seawater at high tide.

Much of the area surrounding the marsh was used for agriculture, while during the First and Second World Wars the marsh was turned into allotments. By the 1950s the area was being used as pasture. But as the water control systems were long neglected, salt water was allowed to flow back into the marsh area. In the 1960s the marsh area became an important habitat for marsh birds and plants and in 1970 the lease on the marsh was acquired from the Pembroke estate by An Taisce, which has managed it ever since as a nature reserve. For the twenty years up to 1970, An Taisce had been campaigning vigorously to prevent development in the area of the marsh.

Two oil spills in the marsh, one in 1982 and the other in 1985, led to the deoxygenation of the area, but it gradually recovered. The vegetation came to be dominated

by *Scirpus maritimus*, a species of rush that could withstand the salty conditions. The rediscovery of a rare species of grass enhanced the conservation status of the marsh.

The status of the marsh means that it has been able to withstand attempts at development in the area; one proposal that got short shrift was a plan for a helipad beside the marsh. In recent years, as the condition of the mud and the water have improved, the *Scirpus maritimus* growth has been substantially curtailed, while many other plant species in the marsh have recovered.

As the marsh's condition has improved, so the number of birds has increased substantially. A wide selection of birds now come to the marsh, sometimes to breed, and well over thirty-five species are now regular visitors. The marsh is an essential refuelling and resting spot for migratory birds and it's an important feeding and roosting area for ducks, geese and waders. The marsh can be viewed from the DART station, although that requires a train ticket, while it can also be seen from the footbridge across the railway line. There's a small viewing area, with seats, at the north-western corner of the marsh, opposite the end of Trimleston Avenue.

The wildlife service plays a monitoring role and must approve any plans for the marsh, while there's also the Booterstown Nature Reserve advisory committee. There are also plans to create a natural heritage area, which would stretch from the Merrion Gates to the west pier in Dún Laoghaire, and out into the bay. If and when this is created, it will give the marsh recognition outside Ireland, while there are also plans to create a special area of conservation covering south Dublin Bay, which would recognise the ornithological importance of the marsh.

ELM PARK GOLF CLUB

Elm Park Golf Club runs from near the main Stillorgan Road to the back of St Vincent's University Hospital; the golf club was established in 1924 when its members got together to purchase Elm Park House and its surrounding lands. A 9-hole course opened in 1925, with an initial membership of 254, and in 1926 it opened its tennis courts. In 1933, the club sold some of its land (which is in Merrion) to the Sisters of Charity for the construction of St Vincent's Hospital, which took a further thirty-seven years to open.

In 1941, when the hospital project was postponed, the club leased back the land so that it could expand the course to eighteen holes, but the land had to be returned in 1956

and the course shrank back to nine holes. It wasn't until 1960, when the club bought the Bloomfield property, that it was able to return to 18-hole status permanently. The final expansion took place in 1994 when extra land was added to the 11th and 12th holes. The greens were redesigned in 2002 by well-known golf course architect, Patrick Merrigan. The Elm Park Stream, which runs through the course, is used to form water features and hazards.

In addition to the 18-hole course, the club also has a driving range and a variety of tennis courts, fourteen in all.

MERRION STRAND

Merrion Strand runs from south of the Merrion Gates for about 0.7km and includes sand dunes with extensive eel grass.

There's a small sandy beach above the high tide mark, close to the railway line. Plant species on and beside the strand include ornamental non-native shrub and coastal marine vegetation.

The strand is a shallow, tidal mudflat and the water depth is shallow, depending on the tides. The strand is in regular use by horse riders, quad bike riders, jet skiers, kite flyers and bird watchers.

OLD MERRION BATHS

The old Merrion seawater baths opened on the strand in 1883; they have been long closed, but the ruins of their outer walls still stand on the strand. The year after they opened, the Merrion Baths and Pier Company opened its pier on the strand; the latticework pier ran for 75 metres, from what is now the main Strand Road as far as the baths. The pier may have been short, but it was the only one ever built in Ireland. The entrance to the pier was through an ornamental arch, which had kiosks on either side. Stalls along the pier sold all kinds of Victorian knick-knacks as well as cockles and mussels dug up from the strand.

The pier was very popular, especially during summer; many people turned out for the concerts given by military bands. The pier also enabled people to get a lungful of fresh sea air, so walking along it was a healthy pastime. Sadly, its popularity proved short-lived and in 1920 the pier was taken down and its metalwork sent to the Hammond Lane scrap yard in Ringsend for recycling. In recent years there has been some talk of reinstating the old pier, but it has never amounted to anything more than just idle talk.

STREAMS

Several streams flow through the Merrion and Booterstown area, all discharging into the sea.

The Elm Park Stream has its source in the Goatstown area, then flows through the grounds of UCD, before crossing beneath the Stillorgan Road and flowing through the Elm Park Golf Club course. It then flows past St Mary's Home for the Blind, enters an ornamental pond and then disappears into a culvert under the Merrion Road and the Nutley Stream. Flowing underneath the railway line, it discharges onto Merrion Strand, 200 metres south-east of Merrion Gates, eventually making its way to the Cockle Lake marine channel.

The Nutley Stream has its source near Beechill, in the south Donnybrook area, and flows underneath the main Stillorgan Road, passing beneath the RTÉ campus, underneath the north side of Nutley Lane, past the Merrion Shopping Centre, underneath St Mary's Home for the Blind, then under the north-east corner of the Merrion Village apartments. By the time it gets to the railway embankment, the Nutley Stream is tidal, finally discharging onto Merrion Strand and making its way to the Cockle Lake marine channel.

The Trimleston Stream has its source just south of St Theresa's church in Mount Merrion, then flows through the grounds of St Helen's Radisson Blu Hotel. From here it flows along the east side of houses in Trimleston Avenue and the west side of houses on St Helen's Road until it reaches the Merrion Road. The culverted stream continues beside the Booterstown Marsh and discharges onto Merrion Strand.

VICTORIA WHITE'S GARDEN

Victoria White, a well-known journalist, grew up at 95 Booterstown Avenue and has fond memories of the garden there. The garden includes part of the Sans Souci estate; this was added to the garden when the estate was carved up in the early 1950s.

Her mother, Edna White, was a keen gardener, harking back to the days of her own childhood in Stranorlar, Co. Donegal. Edna created a kitchen garden in the Booterstown Avenue garden and among the crops that grew in profusion were strawberries, raspberries, apples, gooseberries and greengages. A wide variety of vegetables included French beans, while Victoria remembers that dinners in summer often started with her mother pulling a string of sweet new potatoes out of the ground and boiling them with fresh mint.

12

SPORT

BLACKROCK COLLEGE

Blackrock College has been synonymous with sport, especially rugby, for the best part of 140 years.

The college's rugby football club was founded in 1882 and it went on to become one of the foremost senior rugby clubs in Ireland. In 1887, the Leinster Schools Rugby Cup competition was launched. Since that year, when the Senior Cup team was inaugurated, Blackrock has been consistently successful, as it has with the Junior Cup team, which started in 1909. More recently started competitions include the Leinster Senior Schools Division One league, begun in 1967, and the Leinster Schools' Junior League, Division One, which began in 1978. In 1961, Blackrock Rugby Football Club purchased grounds and premises at Stradbrook, Blackrock.

In addition to rugby, Blackrock has a fine reputation in athletics, where it has had consistent success in such competitions as the Leinster Senior Shield. In tennis, college students have performed well in Leinster competitions at junior and senior level since 1940. Table tennis is played at the college, while Blackrock College has won many swimming and water polo competitions since 1922.

Squash is another speciality, while soccer, Gaelic football, hurling and cricket are all played, in addition to golf, cross country running, basketball and cricket.

While over twenty bishops have been either students of the college or on its staff, Blackrock College has produced infinitely more rugby stars and equally successful stars of many other sports.

Brian O' Driscoll, at Blackrock College from 1992 to 1998, is a former captain of the Irish national rugby union team. Other famous rugby stars with Blackrock College connections include, in alphabetical order, Niall Brophy; Denis Buckley; Joey Carbery; Fionn Carr; Andrew Conway; Victor Costello; Leo Cullen; Conor Deane; Caelan Doris; Luke Fitzgerald; Neil Francis; Jason Harris-Wright; Oliver Jager; Hugo Keenan; Brendan Macken; Hugo MacNeill; Ian Madigan; Niall Morris; Brendan Mullin; Gavin Mullin; Jordi Murphy; Ryle Nugent (RTÉ rugby commentator); Tommy O'Brien; Conor Oliver; Jack Power; David Quinlan; Gary Ringrose; Peter Rob; Mark Roche; Charlie Rock; Alain Rolland; Fergus Slattery; Nick Timoney and Cillian Willis.

Other former Blackrock College students who have achieved high sporting achievements include Nicholas Roche (professional cyclist); Michael Darragh MacAuley; Cian O'Sullivan and Mark Vaughan (all Dublin Gaelic footballers).

Among the many sports facilities at Blackrock College over the years has been the Des Places Hall, opened in October 2012 by the then Papal Nuncio, Archbishop Charles Brown, an American. He was Nuncio here between 2011 and 2017, when he was appointed Apostolic Nuncio to Albania. The new hall is dedicated to Claude Poullart des Places, one of the founders of the Spiritan Order, closely connected with

Blackrock College. The opening of the new hall transformed the day-to-day running of many indoor sports activities.

MERRION CRICKET CLUB

Despite its name, the Merrion Cricket Club has no geographical connection with Merrion, since it's located at Anglesea Road, between Donnybrook and Ballsbridge.

It can trace its origins back to 1864, following which it had several changes of name, becoming at one stage the Irish Land Commission Cricket Club. Then, when it moved to its present grounds in 1906, it became the Merrion Cricket Club. Originally it leased its grounds in Anglesea Road, but bought them in 1950. After 1919, the restrictions on membership were lifted; until then, it had only been open to civil servants.

The club began playing senior cricket in 1926; its golden era was from 1940 to 1963, while the seniors' fortunes revived in the 1990s. During that decade, junior cricket also improved, while women's cricket also came into its own.

ST ANDREW'S COLLEGE

The college, which moved to Booterstown Avenue in 1973 from Wellington Place in Ballsbridge, has long fostered a keen interest in sport among its students.

It has a long history of cricket, going back to its earliest days, and as early as 1901 a pavilion was built for the school's cricketers on the playing fields in Donnybrook. When St Andrew's moved to Booterstown, it also became co-educational and cricket expanded to include a girls' section.

Sport is a big part of student life at St Andrew's and the sports programme is driven by the teachers, who encourage all students to take an active part. Hockey, rugby and basketball are the main sports played in winter, with on average forty teams being fielded across the three sports, at provincial and national level. In winter, badminton, cross country running, equestrian sports, golf and sailing are encouraged. Rugby had its most successful season in recent times during 2014.

The summer programme offers athletics, cricket and tennis for boys and girls with an indoor soccer tournament for boys. Over the past decade, boys and girls have made significant sporting progress at national as well as at provincial level in Leinster. The college is fortunate because all its sporting facilities are on campus; the college has two synthetic hockey pitches, two rugby pitches, a gym and weights facility and a state-of-the-art sports hall.

13

TRANSPORT

ACCIDENTS

A study of road traffic accidents from 2008 until 2012 showed that on the main road between Ailesbury Road and the junction with Mount Merrion Avenue, fifty road traffic accidents had been reported. Two of them were serious, but with no fatalities, while the remainder were classed as minor accidents. Pedestrians were involved in eight accidents, all minor.

BOOTERSTOWN RAILWAY STATION

A busy stop on the DART line, this station has a long history. It first opened in 1835, surviving until 1960. Then it was closed, before being reopened in March 1975 and remaining open until the DART system started in 1984. The station has two platforms, one up, the other down, as well as a footbridge. In 1980, before the DART opened, this footbridge formed the cover image for a pop single created by U2, *A Day Without Me*.

The DART runs every 15 minutes on weekdays, and at longer intervals through the weekend. In 2015, plans were announced to reduce the time between DART trains to 10 minutes, but this has yet to happen. At peak rush hour periods during the week, six or eight carriage DART trains are run.

BUSES

A number of Dublin Bus services operate along the Merrion Road and the Rock Road, including the 4 from Harristown to Monkstown Avenue; the 7 from Mountjoy Square to Bride's Glen on the Green Luas line; the 7A from Mountjoy Square to Loughlinstown, while other 7 services extend as far as Shankill. Two Aircoach routes also use the main coast road service to Dublin Airport.

Long before tram and bus services were introduced on this route, beginning with horse-drawn trams in the 1870s, the usual form of transport was in the shape of horse-drawn jaunting cars.

CYCLE COUNTER

The electronic cycle counter that was installed on the Rock Road, on the approaches to the Booterstown Avenue junction, has shown a remarkable increase in the number of cyclists using the route in recent years. During the first six months of 2016, the number of cyclists increased by 49 per cent compared with the figures for the same period of 2014, and those increases have continued.

Along Rock Road, from Blackrock, there's a dedicated cycle lane, but as the Merrion Road passes through Merrion the bus lanes have to double as cycle lanes, since there are no dedicated cycle lanes.

EASTERN BYPASS

Although this plan has gone very quiet in recent years and wasn't even included in the draft of the city development plan for 2016–22, it hasn't gone away. Sources who are well informed on local government issues say that the plan could still be resurrected. The original plan called for a motorway starting at the southern end of the Dublin Port Tunnel, going through the East Wall Road area, underneath the River Liffey and overground through Ringsend and Irishtown. It would then either burrow through a tunnel between Sandymount and Merrion Strands, or go overground on a flyover. Past the Merrion Gates, a motorway would then gouge a huge swathe through Booterstown, through the southern grounds of the UCD campus, eventually joining the M50 at Sandyford.

If the Eastern Bypass is by any chance ever built, it would mean Dublin city being completely encircled by a motorway.

IRELAND'S FIRST RAILWAY

Ireland's first railway and the world's first commuter railway opened between Westland Row, Dublin and Dunleary, a 10km-long stretch, on 9 October 1834. As the new service quickly gained popularity, trains ran every day from 6 a.m. until 11.30 p.m., every half hour. In addition to first-, second- and third-class fares, there was also fourth class, in open wagons that offered no protection from the elements.

The line went well inland from the coast at Irishtown and Sandymount, until it reached what are now the Merrion Gates. From there to Peafield, just before Blackrock, the line was built on an embankment a little way out from the coastline. Eventually the space between the line and the land was filled in, a process that also helped create Booterstown Marsh.

For well over a century trains on this line were powered by steam locomotives, until diesel started to replace steam in the 1950s. In that decade and in the 1960s, CIE used railcars, which in the early 1970s were converted into a push-pull operation. But by the late 1970s, the 2600 class diesel railcars were in poor condition, providing an uncomfortable and unreliable service.

But at one stage before then, from 1932 until 1949, a very innovative engine was used on the line, delivering a service from Dublin city to Bray, the Drumm battery train. Especially during the Second World War emergency period, it kept the line going when other train services were badly hit by fuel shortages. The Drumm train closed down in 1949, partly because getting spare parts had become so difficult. But in its day it was very efficient, doing the non-stop run from Dublin city centre to Bray in a little over 20 minutes.

MERRION

Merrion had a railway station that was closed down no fewer than four times. It first opened in 1835, then closed in 1862. It reopened twenty years later, in 1882, then shut down in 1901.

It opened for the third time, very briefly, in March 1928, closing little over a year later, in July 1929. It then reopened in August 1930 and stayed open until September 1935, when it closed down for good.

MERRION GATES

The notorious Merrion Gates date all the way back to 1834, when the Dublin to Dunleary railway opened. In recent years the gates have been the cause of ever-increasing bottlenecks as traffic emerges from the main coast road through Sandymount onto the main Merrion Road, or else turns from the Merrion Road in the direction of Strand Road, Sandymount.

Various solutions have been proposed over the years, but none was ever implemented. A plan launched in 2016 ran into a storm of protest from local residents. This scheme sees a new bridge built from Strand Road onto Merrion Road, over the car park to the immediate south of Our Lady Queen of Peace church; this new bridge would take vehicular traffic, while an underpass would be built beneath the DART line for pedestrians and cyclists. The plan would also allow for the completion of the East Coast trail route for pedestrians and cyclists along this part of Dublin Bay.

The 2016 plan for the overpass and underpass was costed at €48 million and was designed to bypass completely the level crossing gates at Merrion Gates. But the planners hadn't reckoned on the strong local hostility to their ideas, even though they only envisaged a small number of houses being demolished. The plan has now been scrapped, although no alternative schemes have emerged.

PEDESTRIANS

The 2016 study of the road corridor from Sandymount and Merrion to Blackrock showed that there were footpaths on both sides of the main Merrion and Rock Roads for the whole duration of the route. However, it said that most of the footpaths had a limited number of pedestrians, although there were significant numbers of people crossing the main road at Booterstown in order to reach the railway station and nearby bus stops at the start and end of the school day.

ROAD TRAFFIC

The Rock Road and the Merrion Road have some of the heaviest traffic volumes of any route in Dublin. A 2016 study of the Sandymount and Merrion to Blackrock corridor showed that around 20,000 vehicles a day were using the route. This study also noted that there was potential for significant growth in the area of the Greater Dublin Area Cycle Network plan. Existing cycle routes include the East Coast Trail and the Blackrock to city centre cycle route. Sections of these cycling routes that have been completed in the recent past include Frascati Road and Temple Hill Road.

TRAMS

The first trams to use the Merrion Road at Merrion and the Rock Road in Booterstown and Williamstown started operating in 1879; they were horse-drawn and ran from Nelson's Pillar, beside the GPO in central Dublin, as far as Dalkey, taking in what was then Kingstown en route. Other tram service started at the same time went as far as Blackrock. It took a further seventeen years before the Dublin Southern Districts Tramways Company introduced electric trams on these routes, in 1896. They continued to run until 1949, when they became the last trams to be withdrawn from service in Dublin, giving way to buses.

WILLIAMSTOWN

Williamstown also had a railway station, albeit briefly. It opened in 1835 and remained open until 10 May 1841.

FURTHER READING

Conroy, Colin, *Historic Merrion*, Merrion, 1997.

Farragher, Seán P., *The French College, Blackrock, 1860–1896*, Blackrock, Co. Dublin, 2011.

Farragher, Seán P., *Blackrock College,1860–1995*, Blackrock, Co. Dublin, 1995.

Fitzpatrick, Georgina, *St Andrew's College, 1894–1994*, Dublin, 1994.

Lyng, Paul, *Booterstown Parish: A Pastoral Journey through Four Centuries, 1616–2013*, Drogheda, 2013.

Lyng, Paul, *Booterstown: A Snapshot of the 1940s*, Drogheda, 2011.

Murray, Paddy (ed.), *Fearless and Bold: A Celebration of Blackrock College*, London, 2009.

Pearson, Peter, *Between the Mountains and the Sea*, Dublin, 1998.

Roche, Tom and Finlay, Ken, *Blackrock, Dún Laoghaire and Dalkey: Along the Coast from Booterstown to Killiney*, Donaghadee, Co. Down, 2003.

Smyth, Hazel P., *The Town of the Road: The Story of Booterstown*, Bray, Beyond the Pale Publications, 1994.